A Family Treasury of Faith

STORIES TO SHARE

Patricia St. John

Harold Shaw Publishers
Wheaton, Illinois

Originally published by HarperCollins Publishers Ltd under the title *Would You Believe It? A Young Person's Guide to Knowing God.*

ISBN 0-87788-820-5

Cover design by David LaPlaca

Library of Congress Cataloging-in-Publication Data

St. John, Patricia Mary, 1919-1993
    Stories to share : a family treasury of faith / by Patricia St. John.
      p.   cm.
    ISBN 0-87788-820-5
    1. Christian life—Anecdotes.   I. Title.
   BV4517.S74 1997
   249—dc21   97-21399
                                                  CIP

04 03 02 01 00 99 98 97
10 9 8 7 6 5 4 3 2 1

To Rosy
to whom these stories
were first told

Contents

Chapter 1

He loves each one of us
as a father loves

Luke 15:11-32

THE WHITE HANDKERCHIEF

The man sat on the pavement beside the bus stop and stared at the stones. A few people turned to look at him—his unshaven face, his slumped shoulders, and broken shoes, but he was not aware of their glances because he was reliving his life. He was no longer a hungry tramp who had slept last night under a railway arch; he was a boy who lived in a small red brick house up the next street, more than twenty years ago. Perhaps they had bulldozed over the house by now; he hoped they hadn't crushed the pansies. It was strange how well he could remember the pansies, and the swing his dad had made for him, and the path where he had learned to ride his bike. They had saved up for months to buy that bike.

The man shrugged impatiently, for the brightness of those pictures hurt him, and his memory traveled on another ten years. The bike had been exchanged for a motorcycle, and he had begun to come home less often. He had a job by then and plenty of friends. Mum and Dad seemed a bit sad and gray, and the pubs were a lot more fun. He did not really want to remember those years, nor the day when the debts had piled up and he had gone home meaning to ask for money. They had made him a cup of tea, and he had not liked to mention what he had come for. But he knew exactly where his dad kept the money, and later on, when his parents went out into the garden, it was quite easy to help himself to what he wanted.

That was the last time he had seen them. He had not wanted to go home again after that, and they had lost track of him. He had gone abroad, and they knew nothing about the years of wandering and the prison sentence. But locked in his cell at night he had thought a lot about them. Sometimes when he tossed awake, and the moonlight moved across the wall, he used to wonder. Once free, he would love to see them again, if they were still alive, and always supposing they still wanted to see him.

When his time was up, he found a job in the town, but he could not settle. Something seemed to be drawing him home with an urge he could not get away from. Every time he went for a walk something reminded him—a clump of pansies, a child on a swing, a little boy running home from school—he could not forget the small red brick house.

He did not want to arrive penniless, so he walked or hitchhiked a good deal of the long journey home. He could have arrived earlier, but twenty miles away he was suddenly overcome with misgivings. What right had he to walk in like this? Could they ever reconcile the haggard man he had become with the boy they had loved who had so bitterly disappointed them?

He bought some food and spent most of that day sitting under a tree. The letter he posted that evening was quite short, but it had taken him hours to write. It ended with these words:

> I know it is unreasonable of me to suppose that you want to see me . . . so it's up to you. I'll come to the end of the road early Thursday morning. If you want me home, hang a white handkerchief in the window of my old bedroom. If it's there, I'll come on; if not, I'll wave good-bye to the old house and go on my way.

And now it was Thursday morning. He had arrived at the end of the street. It was still there! But having got there, he felt in no hurry at all. He just sat down on the pavement and stared at the stones.

Well, he could not put it off forever, and after all they might have moved. If the handkerchief was not there he would make a few inquiries before actually leaving the town. He had not yet had the courage to face what he would do if they were there and simply did not want him.

He got up painfully, for he was stiff from sleeping outside. The street was still in shadow. Shivering a little, he walked slowly toward the old oak tree where he knew he could see the old house as clear as clear. He would not look till he got there.

He stood under the boughs with his eyes shut for a moment. Then he drew a long breath and looked. Then he stood staring.

The sun was already shining on the little red brick house, but it no longer seemed to be a little red brick house, for every wall was festooned with white. Every window was hung with sheets, pillowcases, towels, tablecloths, handkerchiefs, and table napkins; and white muslin curtains trailed across the roof from the attic window. It looked like a snow house gleaming in the morning light.

His parents were taking no risks.

The man threw back his head and gave a cry of relief. Then he ran up the street and straight in at the open front door.

Scripture

As a father has compassion for his children, so the Lord has compassion for those who fear him. Psalm 103:13, NRSV

Let the wicked leave their way of life and change their way of thinking.

Let them turn to the Lord, our God; he is merciful and quick to forgive.
Isaiah 55:7

Prayer

Thank you, God, that you love me more dearly than any earthly parent, for all love flows from you. Thank you for your love that never forgets me, even when I forget you; that always welcomes me back, even when I have sinned; that loves to forgive me, even when I don't deserve it. Thank you for your everlasting love.

Reflection

Can you say for yourself that God loves you?
In what ways are you aware of his love?

Chapter 2 — THE LOST BOAT

*God made us and
bought us back*

*Genesis 1:26–28;
Jeremiah 31:3*

John had spent many Saturday afternoons in the garage, building that boat. He had carved the hull out of a solid block of wood, chiseling it out and sandpapering it. His mother had helped with the sails, but he had a model and knew exactly what to do about the rigging. It was a beautiful model sailing ship, and the best of it was that he had made it all himself.

Now it was finished, and it was displayed in state in the living room, admired by all. His father was especially impressed.

"I am proud of you for being so clever with your hands, John," he said. "What are you going to make next?"

But John had not thought about what was next. His boat was enough for the present.

It was a lovely spring day when he took the boat to the canal to sail it, and he headed for the best place—a little sandy beach, hidden by rushes, where he had once found a moorhen's nest. It was perfect sailing weather, sunny and windy, and as he launched his boat, the breeze caught its sails and bore it out into the amber water of the current. He squatted at the edge and gave play to the string. In a few minutes he would climb the bank and run along the towpath, but first he would just stay where he was to admire its beauty. So absorbed was he that he never heard voices just behind him, and he jumped when three boys a good deal older than himself slid down into the rushes and squatted beside him. He clutched the string tightly, for these were not boys he knew. He thought they probably came from one of the barges that traveled up and down the canal.

"Here, give us a go," said the oldest.

"Well, only for a minute," said John. "I'm just going to pull her in."

He felt nervous and alone, for these boys looked like thoroughly rough types. The biggest lad had already snatched the string from John's hand and was hauling in the boat, pulling it over on its side and drenching the sails. As it approached the bank John found himself suddenly tipped into a bed of nettles and rushes. His hands squelched in the soft mud, and dirt flew into his eyes, blinding him for a moment. When at last he struggled to his feet, spitting out moss and mud, there was neither boy nor boat to be seen, only the trampled reeds and the weeping willows.

He scrambled up the bank, but the boys had disappeared behind the hedges, and he could not even see which direction they had gone. Besides, if he did catch them, there was nothing he could do against three of them, so he wiped his hands and turned home. He knew that his parents had gone out to tea, and he doubted whether the police would be very impressed if he phoned up and told them.

When his parents returned, his father set out at once to make inquiries, but no one in the locality had seen three young strangers. John was very quiet at suppertime, and when he was alone in bed, he found himself crying. His father had offered to help him make another boat, but it would not be the same. This was his first, his very own. He would never forget it.

The weeks passed. John and his father made another boat and sailed it on the river, but John did not forget the first one. Sometimes he would lie awake and remember the shine of the paint and the billowing of the sails and wonder where it had got to.

One afternoon he cycled into town to buy a birthday present for his mother. Having found what he wanted, he took a short cut home through the narrow back streets. He loved the poky little secondhand junk shops, and he dawdled along gazing in at the windows. Suddenly John stopped dead still, for there in the center of a shop window, along with an old guitar and a brass coal scuttle, stood his boat.

Propping his bicycle against the wall, he burst into the shop. "That boat in the window," he gasped. "It's mine! I made it."

The little old shopkeeper looked at him over his spectacles. "On the contrary, young man," he replied, "it's mine! I bought it off a couple of boys weeks ago. I've just put it in the window."

"But I made it. It's mine, truly it is. Please give it to me."

"Not unless you pay the proper price. It's marked on the ticket."

"But I've spent all my money."

"Then you must get some more."

John realized that argument was hopeless, but there was still time. He sped home and found his father gardening.

"Dad," he shouted breathlessly, "can you lend me fifty pence?"

"Why?" asked his father cautiously. "And how will you repay it?"

"I'll clean the car, or mow the lawn, or do anything you want, but I must have it. It's my boat . . . if I hurry, I can get back before the shop closes."

His father looked longingly at his roses, sighed, and nodded toward the car.

"Hop in," he said. "It's nearly closing time. And you'd never get it home on the bike without messing up the rigging."

The shopkeeper was just about to close and put up the shutters when John rushed in.

"I've got it," John shouted. "Now please give me my boat!"

11

"I'll sell you *my* boat," said the old man with a chuckle, handing it over.

The father and son drove home in silence, John examining his treasure. Only as they reached the gate did he speak. "You know what, Dad?" he said. "I was thinking . . . this boat belongs to me twice. I made it and I bought it. Isn't that amazing?"

"Very," agreed his father, "and all the more reason to look after it. . . . "

But John was not listening. He had shot off to show the miracle to his mother.

———◆·◦◦·◦———

So God created us for himself, but we strayed away from him and began to live selfishly, preferring to please ourselves. Sin, our rejection of God, put us under the devil's power. But God himself came to us in Jesus Christ, the God-man, and paid the penalty for all our sins with his own life. *To redeem* means to buy back something that already belonged to you. God redeemed us and can therefore now claim us as twice his own.

Scripture

The Lord who created you says, "Do not be afraid—I will save [redeem] you. I have called you by name—you are mine." Isaiah 43:1

Prayer

O God, my Father and Creator, thank you that you created me for yourself and loved me even before I was born. Thank you for coming to me in Jesus, and paying the price of sin, when Jesus died. Help me to give myself to you as twice yours because you made me and because you redeemed me.

Reflection

Why do you think God still cares about people, even after thousands of years when they have been turning their backs on him? What has kept God from saying something like, "If people choose to go their own way rather than my way, I'll just let them go"?

Chapter 3

THE CLOSED WINDOW

*God removed the wall
between us and him*

Ephesians 2:12, 18

Anna had never really been ill in her life, except for a cold, and she could not imagine why her throat was so sore, and why she felt so miserable. Her mother stared at her when she pushed away her sausage and baked beans. "I thought it was your favorite supper, Anna," she said. "Whatever is the matter with you?"

"Nothing," whispered Anna, and then everything seemed to spin round, and she laid her head on the table.

"You're ill, Anna!" Mummy's frightened voice sounded far away. "Let me feel your forehead! Why, bless the child, she's burning hot! Up to bed with you, love!"

It was a strange night. Anna woke and slept and burned and shivered; every time she dozed she had strange frightening dreams and called out for her mother, who was always there. When the darkness paled, and the birds began to twitter, Anna woke up properly and wanted to know what was happening to her.

"You've got a nasty sore throat and fever," said her mother, who looked as though she had not slept all night. "Daddy's just going to phone the doctor."

The doctor came quite quickly and swabbed Anna's throat and examined her all over. He looked rather grave. Afterward, Anna could hear him talking to her mother in the passage, but she could not hear what they said.

Hours passed while Anna dozed and woke and sipped water, and her mother sat beside her. Then she fell into a deep sleep, and when it was night again, her mother lay nearby on a mattress on the floor. "As long as she is there," thought Anna, "everything is all right. But I do wish this sore throat would go."

Next morning the phone rang, and her father came up to give the message. The swab showed that Anna had diphtheria (an infectious fever now virtually belonging to the past). She must therefore get herself ready to go into the Fever Hospital. The ambulance would call for her in about half an hour.

"You'll come too, won't you, Mummy?" croaked Anna, fixing her eyes on her mother.

Her mother hesitated and looked very distressed. "I'm afraid they won't allow that," she said. "They are taking you away because you are infectious. But I'm sure the nurses will be very kind, and I will come this afternoon."

If Anna had been feeling well she might have enjoyed the hospital, for there were other children in the ward, and the nurses were kind. But her throat still hurt badly, and she felt terribly homesick, so she just lay there, fighting back her tears and watching the door. Her mother had said she would come that afternoon, and Anna wanted her more than anything else in the world.

Then, suddenly, the nurse came over to her and said, "Look, Anna, there's your mother outside the window. Don't sit up now! Just wave and give her a nice smile."

"But," cried Anna, "tell her where the door is! Please let her come in quick. I want to tell her something . . . it's very important."

"I'm sorry," said the nurse very gently, "but no one is allowed in because all the children here are infectious. You don't want your mother to get ill, do you? If you've got a message, I'll give it to her."

Anna shook her head. She had no message, and she was too disappointed to speak. Her strong, comforting mother was there, longing to come to her, the only person who could put things right, but all they could do was to look at each other helplessly through the glass. Nurse would not even open the window. They smiled bravely again to cheer each other up and then waved good-bye. And Anna, who was feeling very ill, buried her face in the pillow and wept because it was just as though her mother had never come.

Time passed slowly, and Anna got better every day. Then a wonderful thing happened. Anna was sitting by the window in her dressing gown, and her mother appeared as usual. But that afternoon the nurse opened the window wide. "Now you can both have a nice talk," she said.

And how they talked! There was so much to tell and hear—a whole week's news. They talked and talked until the sun disappeared behind the trees and nurse told Anna to go back to bed. How sweetly and deeply she slept that night, knowing that there would never be anything between herself and her mother again. Every day now the window would be open.

Now time moved faster, for the weather was fine, and Anna was allowed to walk with her mother in the garden and to play outside with other children. She could look through the railings and see the blossoms in the hedges and the new lambs skipping. She knew it would not be long now before she went home.

Sure enough, the day came. Anna was drinking cocoa at the ward table when the doctor came in with a paper in his hand. "Well, Anna," he said, "you seem all clear. Phone her mother please, Nurse. Tell her that Anna can go home today."

So that afternoon, instead of saying good-bye at the gate, Anna got into the car, and they drove away together. No more windows, no more good-byes! Anna was going home.

———————◆◆◆◆◆———————

God is the source of all life, love, comfort, and happiness. Whatever we may think, we shall never find real lasting joy apart from him. But sin has made a barrier between us. I cannot come to God until the barrier of sin has been taken away.

God has come to me in Jesus, and by his death, he has pulled down that wall. The New Testament says that Jesus took the barrier out of the way and nailed it to the cross. There is therefore an open way to God, and an open way to heaven, for all who are willing to believe that Jesus *is* that Way.

Scripture

Your presence fills me with joy and brings me pleasure forever. Psalm 16:11

It is because of your sins that he doesn't hear you. It is your sins that separate you from God when you try to worship him. Isaiah 59:2

Prayer

O God, I know that you are the only person who can make me truly happy. I know that my sin made a barrier between us, but that Jesus carried it away. Help me to understand that if I trust him, there is no wall between you and me. I can come to you at any moment of the day or night.

Thank you, too, that you are preparing a home for me in heaven. Cleanse me, and make me ready for it when you shall call me.

Reflection

Why did it cost God so much—the death of his Son—to remove that barrier of sin? Why wasn't it possible for God to turn a blind eye on human sin in order to spare the Son he loved so much?

Chapter 4

Jesus is the way God came to us

WHY SHEIK ALI RAN

Hebrews 1:1-2; 2:9-18

Ali, an Arab sheik, sat at his table in his rich apartment. It was a beautiful room looking down on a garden where irises and narcissi grew in the shade of a great twisted mulberry tree. The sheik was master of a large estate. His ledgers and account books and diary of events lay spread out in front of him, and his secretary was hard at work. Sometimes Ali seemed to be concentrating on his books, but sometimes his gaze seemed to stray out through the window to where a little boy was climbing about on the great gnarled boughs of the mulberry tree. Black-eyed, black-haired, and dressed in jeans, he looked like any other little boy, but this was Sadik, Ali's only son and heir, and the light of his father's eyes. That was why the accounts seemed to be moving rather slowly that morning.

Sheik Ali turned the pages of his diary thoughtfully. Important guests were coming that night, and his wife had gone away to a family wedding. Well, no matter! He had plenty of excellent servants. He pressed the electric bell, and the messenger glided in noiselessly.

"Fetch Abdullah and the cook," said the master, and a moment later they stood before him in their spotless uniforms. Abdullah was to go to market and buy all that was necessary. He bowed and withdrew. The cook was to bake and roast and serve up a sumptuous banquet. She inclined her head and left the room.

"Fetch the gardener," ordered the master, and in he came. He was to pick the choicest fruit and flowers. The gardener smiled and went away. He loved displaying the harvest of his beautiful garden and orchard.

There were letters to deliver and interviews to arrange. A wall was crumbling near the sheepfolds, and Ali consulted the foreman. A dozen matters needed attending to, and a dozen servants went quietly off in different directions. The master sipped his black coffee, never moving from his desk. He had no need to move from his desk, only to give orders.

Then, suddenly, there was a loud cry from the garden. The master leaped from his desk and ran to the window. His son had slipped from the branches of the tree and fallen with a scream to the ground. There he lay in a bed of irises, holding up his arms, crying for help.

Ali did not ring the electric bell, nor did he send for a servant. He ran past the messenger on duty, down the stairs, and past the porter. These servants stood open-mouthed, staring at their master as he leaped the stone steps and charged down the path.

"I'm coming, my son, I'm coming," he cried. Finally, stooping down, he lifted the bruised child in his arms, carefully supporting the twisted ankle. And, holding the muddy little figure tight against his expensive suit, he carried Sadik past the porter, past the messenger, past the secretary, and into his own bedroom.

God, our Creator, Father, and Redeemer, and the Source of all life and love, has many servants to do his will. But when God heard the cry of his children who had spoiled their lives with sin, he sent neither angel nor prophet; he came *himself*. We know God came in the form of Jesus because Jesus said, "Whoever has seen me has seen the Father." God clothed himself in a human body and came to us in his Son, Jesus. And the apostle Paul wrote about what God did through Jesus: "God, in Christ, was reconciling the world to himself."

Scripture

Praise the Lord, you strong and mighty angels, who obey his commands. . . . Praise the Lord . . . you servants of his, who do his will! Psalm 103:20-21

Praise the Lord . . . lightning and hail, snow and clouds, strong winds that obey his command. Psalm 148:7-8

In the past God spoke to our ancestors many times and in many ways through the prophets. Hebrews 1:1

Prayer

O God, my Father and Creator, I want to think about your greatness. You are the Lord of the universe and the galaxies and outer space. Your angels and messengers obey your command all the time.

But thank you, today, that when I sinned and spoiled the life you gave me, you came yourself in Jesus. You loved me and came. Jesus became a child like me, so he could really get near to me and lead me to God.

Teach me to love Jesus, for in him I shall find God.

Reflection

In your opinion, what does the fact that God came *himself*, in his Son, tell us about his character?

THE UNRECOGNIZED GUEST

There was a time in English history when England was invaded by the fierce, seafaring nation of the Danes.

They came in terrible ships with dragons' heads on the prow, and they fought wearing steel helmets. Wherever they went, they plundered and murdered and burned houses and churches. The English fled from them again and again until a brave king called Alfred made a stand against the Danes on sea and land. At first he was successful, but then came a time when he too was driven back. So fierce and strong was the onslaught of his enemies that Alfred had to flee from his palace and hide in the forest disguised as a vagabond. A great price was set on his head by the Danish king, and Alfred dared not reveal his identity except to a few faithful followers.

One such ally was a herdsman called Ulfric, who loved his king and would never betray him. Ulfric begged the king to take shelter in his cottage, but he did not altogether trust his wife, who was rather a talkative woman. When the king accepted his invitation, therefore, Ulfric decided to keep the visitor's identity a secret from his wife.

Living in the cottage, Alfred was very sad and would sit for hours thinking about his lost kingdom and trying to work out new military tactics. The herdsman's wife had no use for a strong man who sat brooding. There was plenty of work to be done, and she could not understand why her husband should tolerate such an idle vagabond. When the visitor spoke, Ulfric's wife had no idea that she was listening to the voice of her king. So she waited till Ulfric had gone to the fields, and then she started in on the stranger.

"Now come along, my good man," she said. "There's no need to sit idle. You don't seem good for much, but at least you can watch these cakes on the griddle while I go to the well. As soon as they begin to brown, turn them over, and when they are brown right through, take them off."

Alfred sat by the fire deep in thought. Perhaps he saw visions of victory in the glowing wood. If only he could rally his forces . . . if only they could meet and defeat the enemy just there . . . if only he could meet up with his captains . . .

Suddenly, he was startled by a box on the ear and an angry torrent of abuse.

He woke from his dreams of battle and victory to a strong smell of burning. The cakes were as black as cinders, and the herdsman's wife was very, very angry. "You lazy old good-for-nothing!" she shouted. "Can't I even trust you . . ."

"Hush, hush, woman!" came the scandalized voice of Ulfric, who had just entered the cottage. Then, seeing that she had no intention of hushing, he added desperately, "Hold your tongue, woman. Do you not know your king?"

We do not know what happened next, but we know that Alfred was a gentle, just man and that he was probably very sorry for his carelessness. We know, too, that in the end he gathered his loyal followers, and they met and defeated the enemy. Alfred went back to his palace and ruled for years over his kingdom, a loved and honored king. But he never forgot the kindness of Ulfric, and he took him from the herds and made him a bishop. So we can imagine that Ulfric's wife must have curtsied often to Alfred, the king she failed to recognize when he came to her cottage in disguise.

When Jesus left the glory of heaven and came into the world at Bethlehem, very few recognized God in the disguise of a tiny baby. The innkeeper shut the door on him. Later, his brothers and neighbors thought he was an ordinary child. When he did miracles, they thought he was just a good man. But a few did recognize him as God: the shepherds and wise men, Simeon and Anna, his parents, and later his disciples, some people whom he healed or talked to, and the Roman soldier at the cross.

Scripture

The Word was in the world, and though God made the world through him, yet the world did not recognize him. He came to his own country, but his own people did not receive him. John 1:10-11

Prayer

O God, my Father and Creator, help me to recognize you in Jesus. Help me, as I read the Gospels, to see your glory in Jesus. Teach me to hear the voice of God as I read the words of Jesus.

Reflection

God did not come in the way most people would expect—in glorious, splendid clothes, like a king. How would you have expected him to come? Do you think that even now God sometimes comes to you but you fail to recognize him? In what unexpected way might he come today?

Chapter 6

FOOTSTEPS IN THE SNOW

Janet was thrilled with her family's new home in the country. They first went to visit it in April, and while her mother toured the house and her father and her brother, Martin, explored the garage and toolshed, Janet ran out into the garden. Beyond the lawn the ground sloped to a rockery, and beyond that was an orchard of apple trees in blossom and long, deep grass where cowslips grew. It was there, lying in the grass and looking up into the blossoms, that the family found Janet twenty minutes later.

Her mother laughed. "Aren't you interested in the house, Jan?" she asked. "You can't live in the orchard, you know!"

"Oh, I'm interested," said Janet, getting up. "Can I please have the bedroom that looks out on the orchard?"

"And can I have that funny little attic for a workshop?" asked Martin.

"And can I have the bottom of the orchard for my hens?" asked Dad.

Everyone got what they wanted, and they all settled in. The children never got tired of collecting the eggs from the white leghorn hens. Their father had to leave for work quite early and did not get home till six, so Martin took the hens their breakfast before he went to school. Then Janet gave them their supper when she came home from school. She loved wandering through the long grass and clover and sorrel in the orchard and waiting till the birds had all crowded to her feet, ready to be fed.

In the spring they'll have chickens, she thought to herself joyfully, *and I shall watch them hatch.*

Autumn came, the apples ripened, and the children picked pounds of blackberries. The woods beyond the garden blazed red and russet and gold, and the swallows flew away. The leaves began to fall, and the family lit wood fires in the evening. Then one night, while everyone slept, it started to snow.

The snow came hard and unceasingly for three nights and two days, and the whole countryside was covered. The hens huddled in their coops, fussing and clucking, and robins came to the windowsill. On the third morning Janet and Martin's dad got up early and swept a path to the gate, and they walked to school in the car ruts. The next day would be Saturday, and they would go tobogganing.

Janet came out of school at four o'clock and walked home alone, as Martin had gone off with a friend. She loved observing the silent countryside, the imprint of tiny claws in the snow and, where the wood came down to the road, the tracks of little cloven feet. She could see a yellow light in the west and strange blue shadows on the fields. At home, all was silent, for Mother had gone out.

Janet changed quickly, put on her Wellington boots, and made up the mash for the hens. *How cold and bored they must be,* she thought as she hurried towards the lawn. Then she stopped and gave a little gasp. How would she ever get across? She was small and light for her age, and the snow lay thick and unbroken, much deeper than the height of her boots.

The sun was already setting, and it would be dark when Martin got home. She had to think of some way to get over to the hens. Janet stared at the lawn. Was it just shadows, or were there slight marks in the snow? She could not quite tell in the twilight.

Then she remembered. Martin had given the hens their breakfast; he must have crossed the lawn that morning. Of course it was many hours back and a further light snowfall had almost obliterated his tracks, but at least she could try. Janet set her foot carefully on the first mark, and it sunk in only a little onto hard, trodden snow. If she could reach the next one and the next and the next, she could get there safely.

It was very difficult, for Martin had long legs and enormous feet, but somehow she managed—balancing, stretching, and putting her small foot into the prints one by one, right on through the orchard. Delighted to see her, the hens gave her a noisy welcome, and she cleared a patch for them to come out and gobble their food. It had stopped snowing, and Janet stayed with them till they had all hurried back into the coop. She rather liked their squawking in the vast, awesome silence of the snow.

The journey back was easier because the track was more obvious, but Janet's feet were bitterly cold, and the world looked strange and gray in the twilight. As she came out from the orchard, she saw a broad beam of light shining out from the kitchen window. She knew her mother was home, and she felt very glad indeed. It would be good to take off those boots, have some hot tea, and tell her mother all about her adventure.

The footprints led her right to the door, and she almost fell through it into the warmth and light.

"Is that you, Jan?" called her mother's voice. "Shut the door quick! Isn't it cold? Let's make some toast and have tea together by the fire."

Scripture

For Christ himself suffered for you and left you an example, so that you would follow in his steps. 1 Peter 2:21

Prayer

O God, as I read the Gospels, I can see the footsteps of Jesus like a shining track of obedience, love, truth, and courage. Help me day by day to walk in his footsteps and to follow his example. I know how often I go my own way, but help me today to be a true follower of Jesus, living and speaking as Jesus did when he was my age. And please lead me, in the end, to your home in heaven.

Reflection

Why did Jesus live for thirty-three years on this earth? Why did he become a child, a boy in a carpenter's shop, a man who traveled about and was tired and hungry and homeless? What do you see as the most important point in Jesus' example?

Chapter 7

Jesus gave his life as an example for us

THE MAN WHO WAS DIFFERENT

John 13:1-17

Many years ago, when China was open to foreigners, two young men who had traveled there from a distant land set out early in the morning along a rough country track. On their backs were rucksacks filled with Bibles, New Testaments, and Gospels; they were going to a little market town to sell their books and, if possible, to talk about the living God to people there who worshiped idols.

The men swung along happily between deep green rice fields. After about two hours they reached the outskirts of the market town, an open space filled with people, mules, and wares. The young travelers hesitated.

"They may never have seen anyone like us," said the younger, whose name was James.

"No, but we will show them the books," said David, the elder man. "Come on, I think they have seen us."

He was right. As the two approached, all faces turned toward them, and they were soon surrounded by a curious crowd. Some laughed, some questioned, but no one seemed hostile, and the books were eagerly bought. Although most of the farmers in the market could not read, many had relatives or children who could. A book was a rare and precious object, and these were being offered at such a bargain!

David and James moved slowly through the squalid market. It seemed that everyone was bargaining, quarreling, or trying to get the better of someone else. Beggars whined for coins, and the merchants thrust them aside. The young travelers made for a clump of trees and squatted down among a crowd of people who were eating their midday meal in the shade. As they pulled out their remaining books, one farmer said, "Tell us about them. We cannot read."

What should David tell? How could he show them the living, loving God? Would they care? He looked round on the upturned faces, and he began to speak about Jesus—the One who went about doing good, who taught people to love their enemies, who said, "Blessed are the peacemakers and the merciful, and the pure in heart." The people listened in amazement, and soon others joined the gathering. Warming to his subject, David went on and on. . . .

Suddenly he was interrupted. A man pushed through the crowd, eager and smiling. "I know that man," he announced. "He lives in our village. Come, I will take you to him."

In vain David explained that the person of whom he was speaking had long ago left this earth. The man brushed aside his explanations. "No, no," he said. "This friend of yours, there is only one like him. He will be glad to see you since you know him so well. Come, follow me. He lives in the next valley."

David and James were quite ready to follow; the man's words had stirred their curiosity, and there was still plenty of time. They shouldered their rucksacks and followed him, eating their lunch as they walked. An hour's walking brought them to the village—an open space scattered with tumble-down huts, where pigs rooted in the dust and rubbish decayed by the sides of the track.

A few moments later, the farmer stopped. "Your friend lives here," he said, pushing a child with swollen, infected eyes out of the way. "He will be surprised to see you."

This hut was different. There was no rubbish, and instead of trampled mud in the yard, green things grew. The man who came to the door was different, too. His face was a picture of kindness and simplicity. The child with the infected eyes crept softly to the door and was not pushed away.

"Your friends," announced the farmer. "They talked of you in the market. I guided them." He reached out for the coin James offered and then went away. David and James were left with this gentle stranger, who already seemed somehow not a stranger.

"Come in and be seated," invited the man. "You have walked far, and I have little to offer. I will make tea."

While they drank, the man asked questions. "What are you doing in this out-of-the-way village?"

"We are selling books."

"What are your books about?"

"About God the Creator and his Son, Jesus Christ."

"Jesus?" The man rose up with a strange brightness on his face. "Could it be the same? Do you know him?" he gasped. "Could it be the man I know?"

He went to a box and came back with an old, tattered Gospel of Mark in his hands. "This is the book that tells about my Jesus," he explained, and he seemed to linger lovingly over the name. "Years ago a man sold it to me in the market, and I read it over day and night. Never had I known a man like that! I said, 'He is so good. Will I become like him?' Each day I ask myself, *What would he do if he were here in my house?* Sometimes I think he really is here in this hut, or plowing or harvesting with me, or walking the road to market. Could it be the same Jesus that you know?"

They stared at him, his face so bright, so beaming with love.

"Yes, it's the same Jesus," said James. "There is only One."

"Was I right?" interrupted the farmer loudly, suddenly sticking his head through the door. "Was this the man you were talking about?"

"The man we were talking about is here with us," replied David. "He lives in this house. You were perfectly right."

Have you ever seen a field of buttercups before sunrise, with every flower closed? If you were to come back a few hours later, you would find each of the million golden flowers open and reflecting the sun—not struggling or working, but simply looking up at the light. In the same way, as we look at the perfect, loving life of Jesus in the Gospels, seeking to be like him, we shall gradually be changed.

Scripture

All of us, then, reflect the glory of the Lord with uncovered faces; and that same glory, coming from the Lord . . . transforms us into his likeness in an ever greater degree of glory. 2 Corinthians 3:18

Prayer

Lord, as I read about Jesus in the Gospels and think about him and try to be like him, I pray that you will be changing me into his likeness.

Reflection

How can you be more like Jesus? Carefully make a list of seven simple, practical ways in which you can follow his example in your daily life and show your family that you love them. Then try to concentrate on these ways, starting with one and adding one each day. Once you have struggled through your first week, try to keep going until you can see that your life has been changed because your eyes are on Jesus.

Chapter 8 *Jesus gave his life as* *a sacrifice for us* *Romans 5:6-21*	# THE RING AND # THE ROSES

When Francis was born, no one suspected that there was anything the matter with him. He was just another beautiful baby. Not till he was several months old did his parents begin to wonder and fear. Why did he never turn his head when they came into the room? Why was he never startled when his older sister slammed the door? Why did his rattle seem to give him no pleasure?

At last they took him to a doctor, and they were not really surprised when he broke the bad news to them. "Francis is completely deaf and will probably never speak either."

At first his parents were heartbroken, but as time passed, they found it impossible to feel sad in the presence of young Francis. He was so happy, so intelligent, so eager to discover the world of sight. He learned to understand them by lip reading and sign language, and they learned to understand his own gestures and noises. They sent him to a special school for deaf children, where he discovered all sorts of ways of communicating. And his mother would watch him and think, *How can I be sad? No one could have a happier, better, brighter boy than I do!*

Francis loved birds and flowers and would wander for hours in the fields and woods. No one taught him about God the Creator, however, until his uncle came to stay and brought a picture book of Bible stories. Francis and his uncle came to understand each other quickly. Night after night they would sit together with the book, and by pictures and signs and lip reading, Francis learned how God came down to us in Jesus and how, through knowing Jesus, we can know God. Francis had always wondered about many things—Who made the seeds grow? Who guided the swallows when they flew away? He was glad to finally learn about God.

After looking at most of the pictures, Francis was beginning to know a good deal about the love and goodness of Jesus. Then one night his uncle turned the page, and Francis saw a picture of Jesus hanging on a cross between two other men on crosses. The picture also showed a great crowd of people gathered in front of Jesus. Francis could not understand it; he wanted to cry with anger and disappointment.

Using a white paper heart and black paper heart, his uncle tried to make him understand that Jesus, whose heart was pure and sinless, was dying for the sins of all the other people whose hearts were sinful. But even after seeing the picture many times, Francis could not understand. He knew that one man could die instead of another person, and he pointed to Christ and the dying thief, and nodded. But how could one man die for so many people—all the crowd at the cross, all the people in the street down below? He pointed to the many figures in the picture and shook his head.

His uncle thought for a while. Then he pulled his gold wedding ring off his finger and laid it on the table. He went into the garden where the late roses were still in bloom and gathered a bunch of the withered flowers, their petals spoiled and ready to fall. He sat down at the table and laid a petal beside the ring. "Which would you choose?" he signed to Francis.

Francis pointed to the gold ring.

His uncle shook about ten petals onto the table and gathered them into a heap. "Which would you choose?" he signed again.

Again Francis pointed to the gold ring.

The uncle went on and on, shaking the spoiled, dying petals onto the table and gathering them in a great heap before the shining ring. But even when there were over a hundred, Francis, without the least hesitation, pointed to the ring as his choice.

Suddenly he understood and signed to his uncle to stop. He pushed away the petals and laid the ring carefully on the cross; then he scattered a few petals on the crowd. He knew now that if his uncle picked and scattered every rose in the world, the ring would still be worth far more than the mountain of spoiled petals. And he knew, too, that the shining, sinless life of the man hanging on the cross was precious enough to pay for the sins of all the spoiled, sinful men and women and children in the world. With a bright smile Francis laid his hand on the gold.

Scripture

Everyone must die once, and after that be judged by God. In the same manner Christ also was offered in sacrifice once to take away the sins of many. Hebrews 9:27-28

Prayer

Thank you, Lord, that your life was perfect and sinless, so that when you offered yourself instead of sinners, it was a perfect offering. Thank you that you offered up your love for my selfishness and your goodness for my sinfulness. Help me to understand the meaning of your death. Help me to love you, because you loved me so much.

Reflection

What does the death of Jesus mean to *you?*

Chapter 9

THE SAFE PLACE

*Jesus died to save us
from eternal death*

Romans 5:6-9

The farm lay blazing in the midsummer heat; the harvest was in and the corn stacked, and it would soon be time for fruit picking. The farmer leaned on the gate, gazing at the stubble fields. It had been a good crop, and he had done well on the poultry, too.

Under the haystack Bill, the farm hand, was also having a rest. He had finished his lunch and his mug of ale and was smoking a cigarette. There was half an hour to go, and it was pleasant in the shade of the rick. A warm smell of herbs came from the farm garden; it made Bill feel drowsy . . . he closed his eyes. Bill was asleep.

He woke suddenly, only a few minutes later, wondering where the loud crackling noise was coming from. Then he smelled the smoke and leaped to his feet with a cry of horror. By now the cigarette stump had rolled into the burnt grass, but it had already done its deadly work. The rick was ablaze, and the flames were blowing toward the hen coops and the house.

Bill ran as he had never run before. The farmer would be at his dinner, and they must phone the fire brigade. Nothing could be done about the rick—it had already turned from a smoldering heap to a leaping furnace of flame. But they might save the poultry and the house.

Bursting into the house like a madman, Bill dialed 999. "Come quick," he urged. "It's on the main road—two and a half miles out." He flung down the receiver and found the farmer, pale-faced, at his elbow.

"The barn's caught," he said shortly. "So now it's the poultry and the house. Open the three gates into the meadow, and shoo all the poultry toward them—they'll find their way. I'll get the hose onto the coops and the wall of the house."

Together they fought the flames till their faces were black and their eyebrows singed. The farmer's wife had taken her children to the far end of the paddock and was hurriedly carrying their most precious possessions out of the house in armfuls. She was the first to hear the clanging of the fire bell and to see the engine sweep into the yard.

It took some time to get the flames under control. The rick and the barn burned down into a sodden mass of ashes, but the hencoops, the house, and the stable were saved. The wife carried her baby and all her most precious possessions back into the house, then made cups of tea for the weary firemen. Bill slunk off home before anyone got round to asking how the fire had started.

Out at the coops, the farmer put down the chicken feed, and the poultry came wandering back, squawking and suspicious. He counted them carefully; one family was missing, the white hen and her chicks.

Where could they have got to? The chicks were very young—nine little fluffy balls of yellow down. But during the fire he had seen them running after their mother toward the safety of the open field. He would go and have a look round. Going out to the fields through the main gate in the stone wall, the farmer walked slowly, examining the ditches. When he found nothing, he made for the small stile nearest the blazing barn, and here he stopped short, staring at the ground.

The hen sat in a heap in the gap, her head hanging over on one side, her feathers scorched and discolored by smoke. She was quite dead, and yet the path to safety lay in front of her and the way was open. Why had she sat down and died like that? The farmer stooped to pick her up, and he saw the answer. Out from under her limp wings ran the nine fluffy chickens, alive and cheeping. The farmer gathered them into a box and put them by the kitchen stove cuddled up in a piece of blanket.

His seven-year-old daughter just could not get over it. "She could easily have saved herself, couldn't she, Daddy?" she kept saying. "But I suppose they were too small to run fast . . . perhaps they couldn't see the way in the smoke . . . perhaps they were going the wrong way. Anyhow, she knew the safest place was under her wings, didn't she, Daddy? . . . I suppose she just sat down and called them to come and died instead of them. Wasn't she a good mother, Daddy?"

"I shan't have much time to be a good mother if I've got to bring that lot up by hand," grumbled the farmer's wife. "As though I hadn't enough to do already!"

But the seven-year-old laid her curly head against the blanket and whispered, "The gate was open. The hen could have saved herself, but then she might have left her little ones behind, lost in the smoke. Little chickens, little chickens, I'm so glad you came when your mummy called you, or you'd all be dead. Little chickens, I'll be your mummy instead."

———◆━◆━◆◆━●———

Jesus was sinless. He could have gone back to heaven without dying, but he would have gone alone. We would have remained cut off from God because of our sin, and our separation from God would have led finally to real, eternal death. So Jesus chose to die instead of us, so that he now can call us to come to him and live.

This is how we know what love is: Christ gave his life for us. 1 John 3:16

I live by faith in the Son of God, who loved me and gave his life for me. Galatians 2:20

Prayer

Lord, I understand that you loved me enough to die for me, that I might have eternal life. You call me to come and shelter in Jesus, away from sin and eternal death. Teach me to answer your call. Thank you for loving me; thank you for dying for me.

Reflection

Jesus allowed others to torture him to death for our sake—for the sake of _____ (your name). How can we possibly doubt his love? In what ways could understanding this help you sometimes bear the suffering of others?

Chapter 10

Jesus suffered the punishment we deserve

Isaiah 53

THE FORBIDDEN PATH

J
oy lived in North London, so it was quite exciting when her mother announced one day at breakfast, "Miss Fairfax, an old friend of mine, has moved to a cottage in Epping Forest. She wants us both to go and have tea with her on Saturday. She has got a lovely garden, so you can explore while we have a chat."

Saturday dawned clear and sunny, and Joy and her mother set out in the car after lunch. Soon they left the suburbs behind them and found themselves driving through tunnels of beech trees. Joy stuck her head far out of the window, sniffing the woodsy air. "Oh, Mum," she said, "I wish we lived in the country!"

"Perhaps we shall one day," said her mother, "when Dad gets his promotion. I should love it too. Look, here's the cottage."

Joy greeted her hostess politely but hardly noticed what she looked like, for her whole attention was focused on the garden. She saw a mass of summer flowers leading out to a shining meadow of ragwort, with a pond shaded by weeping willows.

Her mother laughed. "Joy will wake up soon," she said. "She so seldom gets into real proper country like this. Can she explore round till teatime?"

"Of course," said Miss Fairfax. "Go where you like, Joy . . . except don't go up that path between the laurel hedges, because . . . oh, here comes Trixie! Down, Trixie! Don't get so excited! She's a good friendly dog, but she will jump up on visitors. Trixie would love to go for a walk with you, Joy, and we'll ring a bell out of the window when tea's ready, so you can hear it in the meadow."

Miss Fairfax and Joy's mother disappeared into the house, while Joy and Trixie made for the pond. They spent a happy, muddy half-hour exploring, and then they wandered back to the garden. Joy stared thoughtfully at the path that curved away round the laurel bushes. She imagined it must lead to an apple orchard, for she could see some boughs against the skyline. *I wonder why she didn't want me to go down there,* thought Joy. *Did she think I'd eat her apples? Well, I won't . . . but I do wonder what I would see!*

She walked round the rockery, but it only brought her back to the same place. *I really would like to know what's there,* mused Joy. *Perhaps it's some secret or some special animal. . . . I'll just go as far as the curve and peep round. There's nothing as far as that, anyhow!*

She tiptoed down the path. Trixie growled. Joy peered round the corner; there was nothing mysterious to be seen. It led, just as she thought, to a small apple orchard. Whatever could be dangerous or secret about an orchard? She decided she would just tiptoe to the edge of the trees and then run back.

Trixie growled again, but she took no notice. *There's nothing here at all,* thought Joy as she stood under the first tree, looking up. *It's a nice place. I wonder . . .* "Oh, help!"

What she had not noticed was the swarm of bees on the apple tree, so close her curls were nearly touching them. They suddenly rose up in an angry, buzzing, black cloud. Joy screamed and ran, with the bees close behind her. And it was Trixie who saved the situation. The collie ran backwards behind Joy, barking furiously, until the bees drew back. Only one, flying high, pursued her as she rushed through the laurel bushes and burst out onto the lawn.

Miss Fairfax and her mother heard her scream and ran to the window. "Horrors!" said Miss Fairfax. "It's the bees! I told her not to . . ."

But Joy's mother did not wait to hear what Miss Fairfax had told Joy. She ran into the garden, toward the terrified little girl with the great bee buzzing round her head. "Get behind me, Joy," she shouted. "Quick! Hide!"

Joy darted behind her mother, and the bee, alighting on the bare outstretched arm, gave her mother a good sting. It then flew over her shoulder and continued to buzz round Joy.

"He's after me!" screamed Joy.

"No, he's not," said her mother. "It's all over. Stop being frightened. Look at my arm—there's his sting. Bees only sting once. You're quite safe now."

Joy stared at the big red welt that was beginning to rise on her mother's arm. She was shaking and very near to tears.

"It's all right, Joy," comforted her mother gently. "It's all over. But next time, do as you're told."

Miss Fairfax soon extricated the stinger and dabbed the arm with disinfectant. Joy was very quiet while she ate her tea and sat as close to her mother as she could. She kept glancing at the red swelling on her arm, but she did not say anything about it till bedtime, when her mother came to say good night.

"I'm sorry, Mummy," whispered Joy from somewhere down under the bedclothes. "I'll never do something like that again. It was me that ought really to have got stung, wasn't it?"

"Very true," her mother replied. "But all the same, I'm glad it was me."

"Why?" said Joy, appearing suddenly over the top of the sheet.

"Because I love you. Now, go to sleep."

———— ❖ ————

When Jesus stretched out his arms on the cross and said, "It is finished," he meant this: "It's all over. I have paid the price of sin so that you can be forgiven.

By trusting in me, you can stop being afraid of death and punishment, because God only punishes sin once. Look at the wounds in my hands—these will tell you how much I love you."

Scripture

Because of our sins he was wounded, beaten because of the evil we did. We are healed by the punishment he suffered, made whole by the blows he received. Isaiah 53:5

Prayer

Lord Jesus, when I think about all your sufferings and the wounds in your hands, help me to understand how much you loved me. Help me to hate the sin that made you suffer so, for it was I who ought to have suffered. Help me to overcome sin, and turn from it. Teach me to love you, because you loved me so much.

Reflection

You can show that you love God by loving others. What small things could you do today to help other people?

Chapter 11

A LIFE FOR A LIFE

Jesus died to give us his life and his righteousness

2 Corinthians 5:14-21

This is an old story about two brothers who lived in Spain many years ago, when law courts were not so careful as they are now.

Luis and Sebastian were twins living in a flat-roofed white house outside the walls of a little mountain town. Their parents had died but had left them a small inheritance, and the boys lived on in their old home. They were so alike as boys that no one in the town could tell them apart.

As the years passed, however, the boys developed differently. Sebastian held a good job; he was kind, steady, and hardworking, and everyone spoke well of him. Luis was lazy and would not work. Caring for nothing but pleasure, he spent every evening gambling and drinking and often did not arrive home till early morning. In vain Sebastian begged him to leave his bad companions and make a fresh start. Luis just laughed.

It was late one night, with the full moon shining on the white walls of the town, that Sebastian sat at the window, strangely uneasy. His eyes were fixed on the white ribbon of road that led to the city gates. Luis, as usual, had not come in, but somehow tonight his brother could not sleep.

Sebastian spotted the running figure even before he heard the beat of his feet, and he went to open the door. Luis, running alone, pushed past him into the house. By the light of the lamp his face showed deathly white, and his clothes were torn and bloodstained. He trembled so that he could hardly speak. "Oh, Sebastian!" he panted. "Hide me! Hide me! They are coming to take me, and it will be death for me."

"What do you mean?" asked Sebastian, running to the window. Sure enough, a crowd of people was surging from the town gates, running . . . running towards the house.

"We drank too much . . . ," cried Luis. "We fought . . . I didn't mean to . . . He fell back and died. Oh, Sebastian, you must hide me! What shall I do?"

But Sebastian already knew what to do and was tearing off his tunic. There was not a moment to spare. "Put on these clothes and give me yours," he commanded. "Quick! Stop trembling. Now run out of the back door and up into the hills, and don't come back for a long time. . . . Run, Brother, run!"

Truly, they were only just in time. Already the noise of shouting and of pounding feet was at their gate. A moment later, the town guard, followed by an excited crowd, burst into the house and drew up short in front of Sebastian. Wearing the torn, bloodstained tunic, he stood very still, breathing fast, with his hair disordered and dirt on his hands and face. As he was handcuffed, he offered no resistance. Then he walked quietly back to the town jail. A few days later, he was tried and condemned to death for murder.

Nearly all the men of the town crowded into that courtroom to gaze at the prisoner. And when the trial was over and the spectators sat in the wine houses discussing the case, they all said the same thing: "How quiet he stood! He did not say a word to defend himself, nor did he plead for his life, nor did he seem afraid. 'You saw for yourselves the bloodstains on my tunic,' he said. 'I have no defense.'"

"And where was that fine brother of his?" asked some of the spectators. "Why was he not at the trial? He was not at work this morning either. Is he ashamed of his brother, that he lets him die alone?"

No one knew the answer to that one, and a few days later, Sebastian was executed. A life for a life.

Luis hid in the mountain villages for many weeks. He changed his town clothes for a peasant's outfit and worked for a farmer all through the harvest season. At first he never dared leave his lodging; night after night he would wake trembling, dreaming of those terrible running feet. But as time went on he grew bolder. He bitterly regretted killing his comrade and longed to see his brother again. *Perhaps they have ceased to hunt for me now,* he thought. *Next market day I will go down, disguised, to the town and try to speak to my brother.*

Luis had grown a beard and stained his face, and no one could have recognized him. Dressed in peasant clothing he joined a crowd of muleteers and went to market. While the bargaining was at its height, he joined a group of bystanders and started chatting. Gradually he drew the conversation round to the recent murder case. "I hear the wretched fellow got away," he said. "Are they still searching for him, or have they given up?"

"Given up?" replied his companion, turning to him in amazement. "Our militia never gives up! They caught him the same day, tried him the same week, and he died two days after that. There's justice for you! Strange thing is though, there was a brother who disappeared the same day and has never turned up since. . . . Some say . . ."

But no one heard what some were saying, for Luis gave a strange desolate cry and ran from the marketplace. Half-blinded with tears, he somehow managed to reach the governor's house and almost forced an entrance. When the governor appeared to see what the commotion was about, Luis fell at his feet. "You have killed an innocent man!" he cried, over and over again. "It was I, not my brother. Now, take me too, for what have I got to live for?"

The governor withdrew. After much discussion, he returned. "The law says, a life for a life," he announced. "If your brother was innocent, how could we know? His tunic was covered in blood, and he refused to plead. The case is closed. Go, and keep your mouth shut, and see that you make no more trouble."

Then, as Luis turned blindly away, the governor spoke again. "Stay," he exclaimed. "You are the only brother of the executed man?"

"Yes, yes. There is no one else."

"Then I have a letter for you. The prisoner wrote it hastily and left it in my care just before he died. I will fetch it for you."

Seated in the old home where he and his brother had passed so many pleasant evenings together in childhood, Luis wept and wept. It was nearly sunset before he opened the letter. It was very short, and he read it over and over until it was too dark to see the writing and he knew it by heart.

"My dear brother," ran the letter. "This morning I shall die, of my own free will, in your bloodstained tunic. Now I beseech you to live in my clean tunic. I send you my love. God bless you—Sebastian."

And Luis understood. The waster who had lived for himself and fought and murdered must be counted as dead in the prison. The man who had loved and suffered and sacrificed must go on living. It should be so. He sat thinking till the early light glimmered in the room. Then he rose and flung off his dirty disguise. He washed and dressed himself in clean clothing, as Sebastian would have done, and went out to meet the new day.

We have come to realize how Christ, at the cross, took the place of all sinners and died, having clothed himself with our sin.

He now tells us to "clothe" our spirits with the new garments of his love and goodness. When God sees us doing this, he rejoices over us and no longer remembers our sins. For he can then see Jesus living in us as Lord.

To all who accept the lordship of Jesus in this way, God opens the gates of heaven.

Scripture

Christ was without sin, but for our sake God made him share our sin in order that in union with him we might share the righteousness of God. 2Corinthians 5:21

Those who become Christians become new persons. They are not the same anymore, for the old life is gone. A new life has begun! 2 Corinthians 5:17, NLT

Prayer

Thank you, Lord, that you took my sin so that you could clothe me in your righteousness. Help me day after day to show out the goodness and cleanness and beauty of the Lord Jesus.

Teach me to understand how this can be.
Teach me to love the one who died for me.

Reflection

In what practical ways can you show out the goodness and love of Jesus?

Chapter 12

Jesus conquered death

Matthew 28:1-10;
John 20:1-23

THE WAY THROUGH

It was raining in torrents for the third day running, and Margaret, glancing out into the dark evening, felt very troubled indeed. She had motored down from her home on the North African coast to visit friends in the southern town of Fez. But that evening she had rung up home and been told that her mother was unwell. She must try and get home the next day, but if the rain went on like this, the main road would be flooded. When the river rose, the south was sometimes cut off from the north for as much as a week at a time.

Margaret woke several times in the night only to hear the beating of rain on the roof. In the morning the radio confirmed her worst fears. The main roads from north to south were completely flooded. Neither cars, nor trains, nor buses could run.

She studied the map. There was another way—a wild, lonely road that wound up into the mountains. Unfortunately, it also descended into valleys that might well be flooded too. Her friends advised her to wait, but Margaret was anxious, and the weather might get even worse. She decided to try. After all, she could always come back if it proved impossible.

After traveling for about forty minutes into the wild, high countryside, she began to regret her decision, for she was driving into a thick mist and could see little except for the rocks on her right. She was traveling very slowly when she heard the hooting of a horn and saw the lights of another car approaching; they drew up side by side on the narrow road and opened their windows. "What is the road like ahead?" asked Margaret.

"No good," replied the driver in French. "The river has flooded at the bottom of the hill. I'm going back."

Two or three other cars followed, but Margaret could not turn around on the hilltop to join them. The way ahead of her sloped down into the mist, so the only thing to do was to drive to the edge of the flood, turn, and come back as well. Cautiously, hooting her horn, she went down to the plain. As she approached, she heard shouting and the shrill voices of children and felt glad to be near human life again.

The whole village had turned out to watch the fun, standing along the margin of the flood. The river had flowed across the road, a gray swirling waste of water disappearing into the mist. The villagers hailed Margaret with peals of laughter, and three asked for lifts back to Fez.

Still, Margaret badly wanted to get home. She got out and stood on the brink. "How deep is it?" she asked.

"Nobody knows," shouted the villagers, delighted that she spoke their language. "But very, very deep."

"How far does it go?" asked Margaret again.

"Nobody knows; but, without doubt, very, very far. It is a big river."

"Has anyone been across to see?"

"No, no, nobody. Who would be so foolish? Do we want to drown?"

"Well, I'm going to see," said Margaret boldly, and in spite of the warnings and consternation of the villagers, she slipped off her shoes and stockings and locked her car. She took a few cautious steps into the flood, and the water lapped round her ankles. Oblivious to the frightened commotion behind her, she paddled on, trying each step, her heart beating rather fast. On she went till she was swallowed up in the mist and the villagers reported her drowned, but still the water swirled round her ankles. It seemed a long, cold journey, but it wasn't too much time before the mists seemed to be clearing a little up ahead, and there in front of her was the road, climbing up toward the next ridge. Still the water was no deeper than her ankles. A few minutes later she stepped ashore.

Going back rather quicker than she had come, Margaret could hear the excitement on the shore before she could see anything. "Ah, foolish woman!" they cried. "The flood has swept her away. Did we not tell her?"

Then suddenly a great yell went up, and the crowd's consternation changed to merriment as the dripping, bedraggled figure waded in through the mist. A lorry and two cars had arrived by this time, and they were waiting to see what would happen. They hailed Margaret joyfully.

"Is it really possible to go through?" the drivers shouted.

"Perfectly possible," replied Margaret. "It is not above my ankles anywhere. The mists are breaking on the other side, and the road runs high for a long way."

"Yes, yes," called the lorry driver, who knew the roads well. "If we can cross this, we shall reach the highway beyond the floods. Come, Mademoiselle, when you are ready, we will all cross over together."

So, to the cheering of the crowd, the cavalcade passed over with the water splashing round their wheels and came out, laughing, onto the rising road. As they climbed, the mists parted, and a pale sun broke through. At the top of the hill, Margaret turned to look back and gasped. For the gray flood she had feared so much sparkled like a sheet of silver, and over the washed, shining mountains hung a rainbow.

A famous man called Roger Bacon once said, "Men fear death as children fear to go out into the dark." No human being has ever been through death and come back to tell others what happens—except one! Jesus died, he entered into death, and his disciples thought they would never see him again. But they were wrong. Three days later he returned, alive and risen, and showed himself to many of his followers. He was the only one to go right through death and come back and tell us that those who love and follow him need never fear death. Through Jesus, death leads to eternal life with God.

Scripture

Jesus said to her, "I am the resurrection and the life. Whoever believes in me will live, even though he dies; and whoever lives and believes in me will never die. Do you believe this?" John 11:25-26

"I am the living one! I was dead, but now I am alive forever and ever. I have authority over death and the world of the dead." Revelation 1:18

Prayer

Lord, I am so thankful that you went right through death and came back to tell us that we do not need to be afraid. I am so glad that for those who love and trust you, death is just the last part of the way home. Thank you for the joy of those who have gone ahead. Thank you that we shall see them again.

Reflection

Is the resurrection of Jesus something you are convinced about? If you believe in it, how does this affect your life? Ask yourself in particular:

What does death mean to me?

What difference does Jesus make to me as I think about death?

Chapter 13

THE VOICE IN THE DARK

Are you sure you don't mind coming home alone, Rachel?" asked her mother. "I'll tell Bill to come and meet you, if you like."

Rachel shook her head hard. Her father always picked her up on his way home from work, but that afternoon he and her mother were going out. Rachel had been worrying about this for days because it would be nearly dark when she came out of school, and she hated the thought of walking by herself in that little back lane, just before she got home. The trees met overhead and made strange, frightening noises on windy evenings. If she was late, it might be quite dark.

Only one thing would be worse than having to walk down that lane alone, and that was to have Bill, her younger brother, come and fetch her. Bill was extremely tough and feared nothing. He was always teasing Rachel because she was afraid of spiders and cows and other things. If Bill discovered that she was also afraid of the back lane, she would never hear the end of it.

All day long thoughts of the dark lane bothered Rachel and kept her mind from her lessons. Worst of all, though the day had begun brightly, it was clouding over, and the wind was rising. At half past three they turned on the lights in the classroom. Outside, thunder began to growl.

"Will anyone going in for a music exam please stay behind for a few minutes after school!" Rachel's heart sank at this announcement. Her name came near the end of the list, so she would be really delayed starting home. It was almost dark now, and the other children were hurrying to get home before the storm.

By the time Rachel left the building, it was dark and raining, and the street-lamps were lighted. There were plenty of people about, nothing to be afraid of yet. But, as the wind swept round the street corners, blowing the drops in her face, she began to wonder what it would sound like whistling through the branches that met over the lane.

Soon Rachel reached the place where she must turn off the road and into the tunnel of trees. A clap of thunder startled her, and terror overtook her. Even Bill's jokes would have been welcome now. She was sure that evil things, and perhaps bad men, lurked in those shadows, waiting to pounce. She stood rigid, trying to fight down her fears and make a run for it.

And then, above the howl of the wind and the drive of the rain, she heard a voice calling her name: "Are you there, Rachel?" And she knew that voice. With a little sob of relief she plunged into the shadows and hurled herself into her father's arms.

"Steady, girl!" said her father, rather surprised. "Anything the matter?"

"No," whispered Rachel, still trembling. "I just thought . . . well, I just thought you weren't going to be there!"

"Well, I wasn't," said Daddy. "But we came home early and found you weren't in yet. I didn't like the idea of your being out all alone in the storm, so I came. Come on, let's get home quick!"

So they hurried along the lane together. Rachel hardly noticed the wailing of the wind because she was telling her father how she had scored a goal at netball. And she quite forgot the fierce creatures waiting to pounce from behind the trees, because she was holding tight to her father's hand.

———•◦•◦•—◾———

The three days following Jesus' death must have been unbearable for the disciples. After having known him for more than three years, they suddenly found themselves alone, perhaps in danger of being killed themselves. And whether life or death was ahead for them, it would have to be faced without the Master: For this Jesus, whom they had trusted, had failed in his mission and had finally suffered a dreadful death.

It was to very frightened people, then, that Jesus suddenly appeared on the evening of the third day. Standing in the middle of the group, alive and strong, he stretched out his hands, saying, "Peace be with you. Look at my hands and my feet, and see that it is I myself."

As they looked at the pierced hands of Jesus, the disciples finally began to realize that his power was greater even than the power of death.

Scripture

The disciples were filled with joy at seeing the Lord. John 20:20

Prayer

Lord Jesus, I am so glad that you came back from the dead and that you are alive today. I thank you that you are with me any time I feel lonely or afraid and that in the end nothing can really hurt me if I walk through my life with you. Keep me very close to you all my life, until you take me to your home.

When do you feel afraid? Think about that frightening situation, and then imagine the Lord right in it, holding out his hand and saying, "Peace . . . it is I myself."

*Once you have heard the truth about God
and his Son, how can you respond?*

Becoming a Child of God

In these stories, we have tried to understand more about God as Father and Creator. We have also looked at the way he came to us in Jesus, and how Jesus lived to be an example for us, died to save us, and rose again to remain with us through life, death, and eternity.

God has done all this for every single person, and this includes you. Maybe you find these facts too new and difficult to grasp for the time being. Perhaps you feel the need to think some more, to talk with others, and to pray before you know what your response will be.

But, if at this stage you believe these truths, and you genuinely want to become God's child, this is how you can become a Christian:

To become a child of God, a follower of Jesus Christ, I need to
  ✢ repent of my sin
  ✢ believe in Jesus Christ and follow him wholly
  ✢ receive his Holy Spirit into my life, so that the Spirit can help me live as God's child

Repentance means that
  ✢ I recognize my sin
  ✢ I confess my sin to God
  ✢ I turn away from my sin

God is waiting with open arms to receive you as his child.

Chapter 14

*Repentance means
recognizing my sin*

*Job 42:1-6;
Isaiah 6*

WHITER THAN SNOW

Aisha was a woman living in a North African village. Her husband had many goats and a few cows, and she was better off than most of her neighbors. They mostly lived in thatched huts and fetched their water from the village well and washed their clothes in the stream in the valley. But Aisha's house had a flat concrete roof and a stove attached to bottled gas; she washed the family's clothes under her own fig tree and hung them to dry on her own roof. She was a proud and happy woman, for nearly everything she possessed was a little better than what anyone else had. Other people went to market on mules or jogged three or four miles on foot and caught the local bus, but Aisha's husband had an old car, so she drove to town in style.

One cold, dull December day she was coming home from market. For the last half mile the road degenerated into a rough track, but this time she hardly noticed the jolting, for she was looking over her purchases. While most of the village women washed with great yellow bars of soap, Aisha had bought a soap powder that an advertisement claimed would "wash whiter." She loved her children's clothes to look cleaner than anyone else's, and she had a big wash waiting for the new soap powder. She hoped the weather would hold, for a bitter north wind was whistling through the gorges of the hills behind the village. She was glad to get home, call in her children, and put on the kettle.

Next morning Aisha woke early and heated the water. She worked hard, and soon all the clothing was hanging out on the roof for the whole village to see. She looked round contentedly. Across the track her neighbor had spread out some ragged little garments on the prickly pear hedge, but they looked poor and dingy compared with hers. Her powder really did wash whiter.

As the day passed, the weather got colder and colder, the sky over the mountain turned a strange light gray, and the peaks looked near and menacing. None of the clothing was dry by nightfall. Families huddled round the glowing charcoal and went to bed early.

When they woke, the sun was shining, and Aisha gave her children their breakfast and sent them off to school. Then she climbed the outside staircase to look at her washing. Surely it would shine dazzling white in the sun—so white that all the village would turn and gaze at its purity and wonder. She opened the door of the roof and stood as if transfixed.

"Who's been soiling my washing?" she cried angrily, striding forward. Then she stopped again, this time understanding the scene in front of her. Snow had fallen in the mountains during the night, and the peaks behind her home were covered in dazzling white, too bright to look at, at first. Against that sparkling purity, her newly washed, unsoiled sheets looked almost gray.

"Truly, they are nothing to God's whiteness," Aisha muttered, pulling them down in a hurry. But as she turned her back on those shining summits, she caught sight of the rags on the prickly pear hedge opposite and felt comforted.

If you look round and compare yourself with other people, you can always find someone who is less courteous, less fortunate, and less well-behaved than you, and that may make you feel good. When we look at the shining, pure, loving life of the Lord Jesus, however, we cannot feel self-satisfied any longer. Instead, we begin to realize just how far short we fall of his standards. To look truly at Jesus and to think about his life teaches me that I am a sinner.

Scripture

When they measure themselves by one another, and compare themselves with one another, they do not show good sense. 2 Corinthians 10:12, NRSV

Prayer

Lord, as I read the Gospels and look at the love, truth, and goodness of Jesus, help me to see how far I've fallen short of what you meant me to be. Let me stop comparing myself with other people and compare myself with you instead. Make me sorry for all those aspects of my life that are so unlike the life of Jesus, and help me to become a better person.

Reflection

When I read about the perfect life of Jesus, what does it show me about myself? What can I ask God to help me change today?

Chapter 15   THE BARRIER

*Repentance means
confessing my sin*

1 John 1

Zohra lived in a shack near the seashore on the Atlantic coast of North Africa. Her husband was an invalid, and she had no children. She did odd jobs here and there in her town, begged a little, collected driftwood on the beach, and somehow managed.

One year a strange thing happened in that little seaside town. A European doctor started a dispensary in the white house out near the sand dunes, and many people went to him to be treated. Zohra herself decided to go along and ask for a bottle of medicine for her husband because he was much too feeble to go himself.

It was a pleasant place, this new dispensary, clean and quiet. People sat on benches and waited; there was no pushing aside of the poor, no shouting, and no asking for bribes. As Zohra sat patiently by the open window looking out into an enclosed garden vivid with geraniums and nasturtiums, she watched a tiny fair-haired girl toddle out to play under the fig tree. A moment later, her sister, a little older but just like her, appeared in the garden as well.

Watching them, Zohra suddenly had a wonderful idea. These two little girls were playing with the earth; their clothes would get dirty. Their doctor father wore a white coat. Surely the family would need a washerwoman, and surely this dispensary would need scrubbing every day? Forgetting about the bottle of medicine, Zohra slipped round to the door of the house and knocked. A fair-haired young woman came to the door and asked, in very faltering Arabic, what she wanted.

"I have come to be your washerwoman," said Zohra. "I will wash your clothes as white as milk; I will scrub and cook. I will come every day."

The young woman laughed. "As a matter of fact," she said, "I do need a washerwoman. Come back tomorrow when I have talked to my husband."

Zohra went home walking on air. She was sure she would get that job. She and that young woman had somehow clicked, and those funny little girls with heads like yellow chickens had smiled up at her too. As she neared home, though, she saw something even better than the prospect of a job. The gate had been left open at the big house next to hers, and a fat hen had strayed out into the road where it was scratching the dust in a leisurely sort of way.

What a lucky day it was! Zohra looked all round, but there was no one in sight. The hen was tame and friendly and clucked at her feet. She snatched it up, hid it under the folds of her voluminous white *haik*, and hurried into her own little home. Her husband was delighted with the prize—it was a long time since he had had a good meat meal. He lumbered out into the little yard and cut the hen's throat. Zohra plucked the feathers in no time and buried them in the sand. Then she blew up the flames on the charcoal, and soon she had the chicken bubbling in the pot along with parsley, onions, carrots, and spices. Oh, it had been a wonderful day!

After making a few inquiries, the young English woman hired Zohra for a trial period, and Zohra was happier than she had ever been before. She loved the sweet milky coffee that she drank each morning on arrival, and she loved the two tiny girls with hair like chicken down. But one thing she could not understand. Every day as she finished her coffee, her mistress would sit down beside her and read her something about Jesus Christ, from her own Holy Book.

"Does she think I can read or understand at my age?" chuckled Zohra. "Can an old cat learn to dance?" At the start she neither listened nor remembered. She switched off.

But the Word of God is alive and powerful and has a way of piercing through indifference or closed ears. After a few weeks Zohra found herself remembering things she did not even realize she had heard: that story, for instance, about five thousand people all feasting off of five loaves and two fishes! That was a splendid story, which she told to her husband. Then there was one about a sheep that got lost. . . .

Very gradually Zohra found herself looking forward to these stories and feeling hungry and restless if she had to miss them. Almost without realizing it, she was beginning to love the One who had healed the blind and raised the dead. And even more slowly she was coming to understand that he was still alive, there, invisible beside them as they read about him. He was there in the house where he was loved and welcomed, and because of him there was peace and gentleness and laughter in that home. Zohra loved being there and hated to leave. She wanted him with her all the time, and her mistress never got tired of telling her that he wanted her. It almost dazed her to think of it.

Then, one summer evening when her husband had dragged himself to the sidewalk cafe, Zohra sat on her step and looked out over the quiet sea. The One who healed seemed near, and she knew now what she had to do—ask him into her heart and commit herself fully to his way. Perhaps she would do it right there . . . but, even as she made the decision, her mind filled with the picture of a white hen clucking in the dust, and the smell of chicken stew.

If we confess our sins, he is faithful and just to forgive us our sins, and to cleanse us from all unrighteousness. Her mistress had taught her that. Zohra's joy faded, for somehow she knew that that little white hen stood as a barrier between her and her Lord, and she could not get past it. Everything was spoiled. She went indoors and quarreled with her husband and could not sleep.

Then the most amazing thought came to her: she could do something about the barrier. She had never heard of anyone doing such a thing before, but she supposed it could be done. On Friday when her mistress paid her, she would get rid of that wretched little white hen.

On Friday Zohra got home early, dressed herself in her best clothes, and slipped through the gate into the little poultry farm. She knew the man would be at work, but it was the woman, her neighbor, whom she wanted to see. Once inside the house, she sat beside her neighbor on a low mattress. With her hands clasped and tears streaming down her cheeks, Zohra told her story.

As she finished, she pleaded, "Oh, my sister, forgive me! I will buy you a turkey or a duck, or anything you want . . . only forgive me."

The woman was staring at her in amazement. The hen and even the money were temporarily forgotten in the sheer craziness of what was happening. "But I'd never have known!" she gasped. "Why, why, oh *why* did you come and tell me?"

"One day," whispered the trembling woman, "one day I will tell you, but not now."

She slipped the price of the hen into her neighbor's hand and hurried home. She had an appointment to keep, and there was no barrier now.

Scripture

If we confess our sins to God, he will keep his promise and do what is right: he will forgive us our sins and purify us from all our wrongdoing. 1 John 1:9

Prayer

Lord, I know that you cannot cleanse what I hide, so I want to tell you about the wrong things in my life that I can remember. Thank you that as I confess them, you have promised to forgive. Thank you, too, for forgiving me those sins I have forgotten about. If I have wronged another person, help me to put it right with them as well as with you. If I have taken what is not mine, help me to give it back. If I have told a lie, help me to say that it was not true. If I have quarreled or hurt anyone, help me to say I am sorry.

Reflection

Make a point of carrying out what you have just prayed for, trusting God to give you courage to go beyond remorse to repentance.

THE FIVE-FINGER PRAYER

Chapter 16

Repentance means turning from sin to Jesus

Luke 15

ndrew had been traveling for hours through the backwoods of northern Canada, and he was tired when he reached the little log hotel where trappers and company officials put up on their journeys. He loved these drives, mile after mile through the green gloom of great trees. He was on his way to preach at a settlement farther north, and he welcomed the thought of a quiet evening.

But it was not to be. No sooner had he signed in than the hotel manager came towards him with outstretched hands. "Pastor Jackson," he said, his face beaming. "They told me up at the settlement that you'd be coming through today. It's real good to have you. Come in for a hot drink."

Andrew could not refuse such a warm invitation, so, sitting beside the proprietor, he heard the man's story. He explained how as a Christian couple too isolated to attend any church regularly, he and his wife were delighted at the coming of a pastor. The family begged him to have supper with them, and over the table the host suggested that perhaps he should invite the few guests in the hotel to stay for family prayers after breakfast the next morning.

"I should be glad to lead them," said Andrew. "But I should like your staff to come, too. As I went up to my room earlier I passed a cleaning woman with such a sad face. When I greeted her, she turned quickly away to wash the window, but I can't forget the sorrow in her eyes."

"Oh, her!" said the proprietor thoughtfully. "She is of Indian origin and has had great tragedies in her life. I really keep her out of pity, for she has lost the will to work. I don't think I could bring her in with my guests; she never bothers to look clean or tidy."

"Let her sit just by the door, if she will," urged Andrew. "I should like her to be there."

Next morning the guests were surprised when a short service was announced after breakfast, but most stayed because in their lonely travels, they likewise were seldom near a church. They listened politely, and a few thanked the pastor warmly, but only one stayed to question him—the sad-faced woman who had sat unnoticed in the doorway. When the other guests had left the dining room, she followed Andrew into the passage.

"Sir," she whispered, "I never heard it put like that before. Could you teach me a little prayer? I'm not educated, you know, but I should like to pray."

"Yes," replied Andrew gently. "I will teach you a prayer. You must say it every day till I return in a week's time, and then I will see you again."

"A very short prayer, Sir. I'm no scholar and I can't remember much. It must be very short."

"It is very short; it is just five words, one for each finger of your hand so that you cannot forget it. Say them after me . . . one word for each finger: *O Lord, Show Me Myself.*"

The pastor drove off into the deep forest, where he was gone for a week. When he returned, he greeted his host and then inquired after the cleaning woman. At this, the proprietor sighed and said, "She seems a lot worse than she was before; every time I see her she is crying into her bucket. I shall have to get rid of her if she goes on like this. It upsets the others."

Andrew went searching and found the woman going about her duties. "Well," he said, "I've come back. Did you remember the prayer, and did you say it?"

The tears sprang to her eyes, and she clasped her hands. Then she whispered, "Every day I have said it, and every day it gets worse; every day I remember more wrong I have done, and every day my heart gets heavier. Oh, what shall I do?"

"I will tell you what to do. Do not pray that prayer anymore at present. I am going to teach you another one."

"Just a short one, Sir. Don't forget, I'm no scholar. I can't remember much."

"It's a very short one—just five words again, like the last one, one word for each finger of your hand. Say it after me: *O Lord, Show Me Yourself.*"

"And for how long shall I say this prayer, Sir?"

"You can say it every day for the rest of your life."

Some years later, Andrew visited that district again to preach in a new church opened near the settlement. Almost everyone attended, and the visitor was particularly struck by the bright faces of the young people and the way they sang. When he commented on it, the new pastor said, "Yes, I'm very thankful for our young people. They have mostly been brought in by a couple living in the district. The two married not long ago, and they do wonderful work among the children and teenagers. The wife is like a second mother to them all. It's a strange story. She is of Indian origin and has very little education. . . ."

"I should like to meet her," said Andrew.

A dark-haired woman dressed in attractive clothes stepped forward, smiling, and clasped his hand. "Do you remember me, Sir?" she asked. Then, seeing the doubt in his face, she laughed. "I did not expect you to recognize me," she said. "But you will remember the prayer, one word for each finger."

Recognition dawned in Andrew's eyes, but she went on speaking eagerly.

"I've prayed that prayer every day since you left me. He's shown me himself, and I am learning to love him more and more . . . Oh, Sir, I shall go on praying that prayer every day till I see him."

———————⚬⬦⬧⬦⚬———————

This woman not only saw her sin and confessed her sin, but she turned from her sin to Jesus. Because she knew that all her wrongdoing of the past was forgiven, she left the old, sad ways behind her and started on a new life. Now she was filled with joy, for she was free to look, not behind, but ahead.

Scripture/Prayer

Remove my sin, and I will be clean; wash me, and I will be whiter than snow. . . . Close your eyes to my sins and wipe out all my evil. Create a pure heart in me, O God, and put a new and loyal spirit in me. Psalm 51:7-10

Examine me, O God, and know my mind; test me, and discover my thoughts. Find out if there is any evil in me and guide me in the everlasting way. Psalm 139:23-24

Reflection

What is the important two-part lesson we can learn from this story?

Chapter 17

THE CAPTAIN AND THE CABIN BOY

Conversion means repenting and believing in the Savior

John 3:1-16

Captain Brown lived in the day of sailing ships, and his beautiful winged vessel was one of the finest in the Merchant Navy. He had sailed in his trading ship all round the world, earning a reputation for daring and iron discipline. His crew were a foul-mouthed, hard-drinking lot who feared nothing. You needed to be tough to sail with Captain Brown or you did not last long.

There came a day when, though the captain was as dauntless as ever, some whispered that he was past his time and should be put ashore. They whispered very softly, of course, for had he heard them he would have pitched them overboard. No one was going to tell Captain Brown when to retire.

His vessel, the *Golden Eagle*, was setting out on a calm Atlantic Ocean one summer's day. Thinking it should not take long to cross with a favorable wind, the captain said to himself, *Then I'll consult one of those American doctors, maybe; I'm not feeling as good as I ought to. But shore's an unhealthy place, and maybe these sea breezes'll put me to rights during the crossing.*

But the sea breezes did not help, and after a few days he found he could no longer bark out his angry orders—he was too short of breath. And climbing up into the crow's-nest made him so giddy that he decided not to risk it again. He retired into his cabin, growling like an angry old lion, and sent for the first mate.

"You'll have to take over for a day or two," mumbled the captain irritably. "Just a touch of bronchitis! The sea breezes will put me on my feet in no time."

But he slept little that night, so in the morning the ship's doctor came to see him. He told him to rest for a few days and he would feel better soon. Outside the cabin, however, the doctor shook his head at the first mate. "I don't think the old man will reach shore," he said. "His chest is terribly congested, and pneumonia is setting in. Ah well, perhaps it's for the best. He'd lie easier in the ocean than under the earth—never was much of a landlubber."

Inside the cabin Captain Brown also knew quite well that the sea breezes would never revive him. In a way he was not sorry, for he had always wanted to die at sea. All the same, he found it hard to face that it was all over for him. For the first time in many years he began to wonder what would happen next. If there was a God, he was in no state to meet him, and he began to worry. Had he been ashore, he could have gone to church or sent for a parson or borrowed a Bible. But here on his own ship, if he'd found any of his crew reading a Bible, he'd have tossed it into the sea. Where could he turn for help?

The captain dozed all day haunted by strange dreams, and, waking in the evening, he knew that he was worse. His worry increased. When the first mate came in for orders, he asked abruptly, "Has anyone on this ship got a Bible?"

The first mate stared. *The old man's delirious!* he thought to himself.

The captain drew himself a little farther up on the pillow. "I said," he gasped angrily, "has anyone on this ship got a Bible? Can't you give a straight answer to a straight question?"

"N-n-no, Sir, I don't suppose so," faltered the first mate. "I could go and ask, Sir, if you like."

"Go!" bellowed the captain. "And don't come back without one."

When the crew heard that the captain wanted a Bible, they thought it a great joke. But the first mate was in no laughing mood. He feared the captain's wrath.

"What does he think we are?" shouted one sailor. "A Sunday school?" But this started a new train of thought. He considered a moment. "Just a minute," he said. "Talking about Sunday school . . . there's that little new cabin boy, Jo Prescott. I've seen him down among the hammocks reading something. Delicate little chap he looks, but he works well. . . ."

"Fetch 'im," barked the first mate, and a moment later Jo Prescott, cabin boy and youngest member of the ship's crew, stood quaking in front of the officer.

"Jo Prescott?"

"Y-yes, Sir."

"I hear you have been seen reading down among the hammocks."

"Only when my work's done, Sir."

"What do you read?"

"My Bible, Sir."

"I see. Well, fetch your Bible, and take it straight to Captain Brown's cabin. Say I sent you, and *hurry!*"

The child's face turned rather white. He was terrified of the captain, but there was nothing to do but obey the order at a run. He had another fear, even worse than his fear of the captain. Supposing they took his Bible away from him?

Jo hurried across the deck, clasping his precious book, and knocked at the cabin door. It was not the usual gruff bark that bade him enter, but a weary, breathless voice. And the spent figure lying on the bed was quite unlike the angry, blustering Captain Brown he had known. Jo's fear gave place to a great pity as he stood at attention waiting for the captain to speak.

"Who are you?"

"Jo Prescott, Sir. Cabin boy."

"Who told you to come?"

"First mate, Sir. He told me to bring my Bible."

"Ah yes, a Bible!" The tired voice was eager. "Sit down, boy, sit down! I can't read myself. . . . My sight's gone dim. . . . Read me something out of that Bible. . . . I may never reach port."

Jo thumbed nervously through his Bible, well aware that the old man was very ill. He came at last to John, the third chapter, and read the story of Nicodemus, who longed to see the kingdom of God. He read slowly and distinctly, but the captain's eyes were closed and his face showed no sign of understanding. When Jo came to verse 16, he read it very slowly indeed. "For God loved the world so much that he gave his only Son, so that everyone who believes in him may not die but have eternal life."

The captain opened his eyes and stared. Jo was emboldened to speak. "Please, Sir," he said. "May I read that verse in the way my mother told me to read it?"

"Read it anyhow you like, boy," said the captain. "Only get on! The time may be short."

Jo read the verse again: "For God loved Jo Prescott so much that he gave his only Son, so that if Jo believes in him, Jo may not die but have eternal life."

The captain had turned toward him. His eyes were fixed on the child, and he was breathing very fast. "Read it again, boy," he whispered. "Read it again . . . and put your captain's name into it."

So Jo read it again: "For God loved Captain Brown so much that he gave his only Son, so that if Captain Brown believes in him, Captain Brown may not die but have eternal life."

"That's it." murmured the captain. "That's the anchor! That'll get me into port!"

So Jo Prescott slipped away, his precious Bible hidden under his uniform, and the old captain turned his face toward the heavenly harbor.

We have seen how God came down to us in Jesus, and died to pay for the sins of the world, and rose again to be our Savior and Friend.

None of this will be of any help to you, however, unless you come to him with *your* sin and believe in him as *your* Savior and Friend.

Scripture

For God loved _____ (your name) so much that he gave his only Son, so that if _____ believes in him, _____ may not die but have eternal life. John 3:16

Lord, I know that you loved the world and died to save sinners from their sin. And I know that you love *me*. So today I bring *my* sin to your cross. I want to confess it and turn away from it. I want to be forgiven.

I take you now as *my* own Savior, and I give myself to you to be yours forever. I put my own name into that verse.

Reflection

Do you feel that you can say with both your heart and your mind, "The Son of God . . . loved *me* and gave his life for *me*"? Galatians 2:20

Chapter 18

*We receive the
Holy Spirit*

John 14:15-23

THE KNOCK ON THE DOOR

Maggie had lived all her married life within sight of the great castle on the hill. Her husband, Robbie, had brought her to this cottage on the riverbank as a bride, and here she had borne and reared her family. Soon after her arrival, Prince Albert had rebuilt the castle of true Scottish granite. The massive tower surmounted by a turret dominated the landscape, looking at a distance as though hewn out of one solid rock. Behind it rose the peak of Craig-gowan, and in front the royal acres sloped gently down to the banks of the Dee. The neighbors considered Maggie a fortunate woman, for her husband was chosen to work as gardener on the royal estate, and he brought home good wages regularly.

"She's a guid mistress for all she's a queen," Robbie would often say when he came home at night, and Maggie and the bairns would gather round and ask questions. When the royal family was in residence, what tales he had to tell!

They nearly always came up in the summer when the hills were purple with heather and the rowans beginning to turn. Then in the evenings Robbie and Maggie and the children would sit on the bench and on stools in the porch—the honeysuckle porch that looked west toward the sunset—and the father would smoke his pipe and recount every detail of his day: the wee princesses had been skipping in the garden . . . No, Daddy was never very good at remembering what their dresses looked like . . . and those bonny princes in their kilts had ridden out with their father, the prince consort. Her Majesty, still a young woman in those early days, often walked in her gardens, and she always greeted Robbie and inquired after his wife and bairns.

Sometimes they had parties, and Robbie would tell of carriages and plumes and beautiful ladies. Sometimes he would be told to carry flowers to the castle, and then he would catch a glimpse of what the cooks were doing. Little Andy, who was fat and greedy, liked hearing about that best of all. How they would laugh at him, sitting on his father's knee, sniffing and licking his lips over imaginary banquets.

Those happy years passed quickly. Then, when Prince Albert died, the queen seemed to grow old overnight, and there were no more gay parties and balls at Balmoral Castle. Robbie still worked in the castle gardens as faithfully as ever, until one winter day when he came home coughing. He died of pneumonia just before Christmas and was buried under the snow. The queen grieved for her gardener. She sent a letter of appreciation about him to his wife, who had joined her in widowhood. She also arranged a pension for Maggie, and this was a great comfort.

The children grew up and left home one by one to marry in other glens or to work in the cities. They begged their mother to go and live with one of them, but she could not tear herself away from the cottage and the castle and Robbie's grave. So they often visited her instead. It was only sometimes, in winter when the roads were blocked with snow, that Maggie had to stay alone with her thoughts and her rheumatism.

Then there came a ferocious winter. No one in the village remembered such cold weather. Snowbound for days on end, the villagers found that food and fuel for the fire were scarce and expensive. Maggie had her pension, but somehow it had melted away in the cold season. The roof had leaked, so she had had to get it mended, and she had paid a laddie twice to shovel the snow from her path. Now, for the first time ever, she was in debt, and she dared not go on buying food at the village store when she could no longer pay for what she had already bought. The oatmeal barrel was nearly empty, and so was the flour bin. Her fire burned low, but she dared not put on more coal. Maggie's heart was as gray and desolate as the low skies over the snow. "Oh, Robbie, Robbie," she cried. "If you hadna' left me it wouldna' been like this."

A knock at the door made her start. Whoever would call on a day like this? An awful suspicion crossed her mind—maybe it was the grocer himself come up to ask for payment of her bill. Shame swept over her. She could not face the respectable Mr. Macpherson and tell him that she could not pay for ten days at least. She would slip into the back kitchen and close the door. After a while he would surely go away, and in this weather he would not be likely to call again in a hurry.

Another knock, rather peremptory. Maggie was glad she had drawn the curtains. She rose and tiptoed into the kitchen, laughing a little. She would not go to her own front door unless she pleased. No one could force her.

And yet . . . standing behind her kitchen door her heart smote her. Just supposing it was someone in trouble! There was Mrs. McPhail up the hill whose wee Jeanie was so sick. Suppose she was knocking on the door to say Jeanie had died? Or suppose it was some poor body in the snow needing shelter?

Another knock, much louder! Maggie ran across the parlor, flung open the door, and nearly fell backwards in surprise. There was a fine carriage in the street, and all the neighbors were at their doors wrapped in shawls and curtsying. On her own doorstep stood a footman in royal livery carrying a great basket, while Her Majesty herself, small and regal, smiled and nodded from the window of the carriage.

Just a few words of sympathy and a sentence of appreciation for Robbie's years of service, and the horses plodded on to another cottage. But the great basket had been lifted over the threshold, and in it was all Maggie would need for a long time to come. Still, it was not the warm shawl nor the packet of tea nor the oatmeal nor the substantial gift of money that brought the tears coursing down Maggie's furrowed cheeks. It was something else.

"She came herself?" murmured Maggie over and over again. "Her Majesty came herself and I never kenned. Thank the Lord, oh, thank the good Lord, I opened the door."

------◆◆◆◆◆◆------

The queen stopped for a few minutes at Maggie's door, but God's Holy Spirit, whom Jesus promised to his disciples before he left this earth, wants to come into our hearts and stay there forever. The Holy Spirit loves to dwell in a clean, forgiven heart. Through his new life we are born again. Through his new life we can grow as Christians.

Scripture

I will ask the Father, and he will give you another Helper, who will stay with you forever. John 14:16

Listen! I stand at the door and knock; if anyone hears my voice and opens the door, I will come into his house. Revelation 3:20

Prayer

"Oh, come to my heart, Lord Jesus,
There is room in my heart for you."—Emily Elliot

Reflection

Are you aware of the Holy Spirit working in your life?
In what particular ways are you learning to recognize his voice?

Chapter 19

THE FRIEND WHO REMEMBERED

The Trinity—Father, Son, and Spirit—makes us new

2 Corinthians 5:14-21

Bruce and Peter were great friends. They sat side by side at school and usually did their homework together, too. Bruce was rather brighter than Peter and liked to help him. In holiday time they went train spotting together and shared a small garden plot and sold vegetables privately to their friends. They were both only children, and their mothers grew used to having two boys instead of one. Mostly, though, they went to Bruce's house because Peter's home was not a happy one; his mother was so taken up with her own troubles that she sometimes hardly seemed to notice her son.

The years passed. Bruce came top of the class, but Peter had to repeat a year. It was not quite so easy to be together anymore, and although Bruce wanted to help, Peter did not seem to want to bother. Besides, Bruce had to work hard for his own exams. Gradually they drifted apart.

Bruce went to college and took up law. Peter tried job after job, but he seemed unable to make a success of anything, and his father nagged him so much that he no longer went home. He took a room downtown next to his favorite pub and lived as best he could. He married at one point, but his wife soon tired of his ways and left him. Years passed, and when Bruce was appointed a local magistrate and moved with his family into a large house on the hill behind town, Peter decided not to go and call.

But the two boyhood friends were destined to meet again anyway, for the law had its eye on Peter. On one or two occasions he had been taken to the police station for being drunk and disorderly, and there had been other little incidents too. He had a small job but found it hard to pay the bills and have enough left over for his drinks and cigarettes, so he had taken to shoplifting—just a little at a time from the food counters. He was very careful and had never been caught.

Then one day the police accosted him just outside Marks and Spencer's and asked to look in his bag. The only thing that bothered him at the time was losing those sausages to the police; he had been looking forward to frying them for supper.

Peter had been to court before. It did not worry him too much, for somehow he felt so tired these days that nothing seemed worth worrying about except not having enough to drink. No one else cared, so why should he? Only one thing really bothered him, and that was the thought of meeting Bruce. *But maybe it will be someone else,* he said to himself. *And even if it is him, he's probably forgotten me.*

The man in the courtroom was not someone else, however. There Bruce was, all togged up in his best suit, and there was no telling whether he had forgotten his old friend or not, for Peter made a point of not meeting those steady gray eyes that he remembered so well. *Only person who ever really bothered about me,* Peter thought to himself rather vaguely, while the faraway voice pronounced his fine. It was a larger fine than he had expected. He would never get it together. Oh well! Prison would be a change!

Feeling rather bitter, Peter let himself into his dingy room later that evening. He had sometimes dreamed of sprucing himself up a bit and going to call on Bruce, but this was the end to that little flight of fancy. He suddenly hated his old friend. He could have got him off if he had wanted to—extenuating circumstances, and all the rest of it; but Bruce had done his worst. He went to the cupboard and deliberately tore up the little packet of letters that had lain there for such a long while. It represented several years the two friends had written to each other after leaving school.

Peter flung himself down on the bed and gave way to bitter thoughts. He did not switch on the light, and it was quite dark when he heard the knock. "If it's the old girl for the rent, it's not due for another three days," he muttered and took no notice. But whoever it was went on knocking, rather a timid knock, not at all like the impatient *rat-tat-tat* of his landlady. He got up, switched on the light, and opened the door.

There was a long silence. "Can I come in, Pete?" asked Bruce at last.

"Please yourself," answered Peter. He was staring at his friend. Without his collar and tie, Bruce looked different. He was just an ordinary man in a polo-necked pullover, broader and graying a little, but not unlike the bright-faced boy who had helped him with his maths. "Make yourself at home," Peter added.

"Thanks," said Bruce.

There was another silence, broken at last by Bruce. "Pete, do you remember that garden plot?"

"You bet. Have a drink?"

"Thanks."

Another silence while Peter uncorked a bottle. It was easier to talk while they sipped their drinks.

"Pete, do you have a job?"

"Job? No. Jail's my next job. How d'you imagine I'll pay that fine?"

"Well, that's what I came about. The fine's paid, Peter . . . and . . . I've been thinking about my garden now. I can't cope with it. It's much too big, and it's gone to ruin. You were always a much better gardener than me, Pete. D'you

remember how the slugs made for my lettuces, and I could never think why? . . .
I just wondered . . . There's a little bungalow adjoining the house, and if you
moved there to work for us, you could do market gardening in quite a big
way. It would be fun to be together again. Would you consider it?"

"How do you know I wouldn't steal your wife's diamond tiara?" retorted Pete,
but he chuckled. He had always loved gardening.

"When will you come?" asked Bruce. "Tomorrow?"

"I'll think about it," said Peter. "Thanks a lot."

He stood at the window and watched Bruce drive off into the rain, but his
thoughts were already busy. He knew the garden; he had often looked over
the hedge and imagined what he would make of it. There was a sunny wall
ideal for fruit trees, and a sheltered bed where he could put in strawberry
plants. . . . He stood for a very long time at that window, just staring, but he
wasn't seeing the blurred streetlamps or the rain bouncing on the pavement.
He was standing in early autumn sunshine, surrounded by the bittersweet smell
of chrysanthemums. . . . He was watching the butterflies on the Michaelmas daisies.

In this story, the judge who condemned and the man who paid the debt and
the friend who gave Peter a new start in life were all the same person. He was
actually following the pattern of God. One day God will judge and punish sin,
and, because he is a righteous judge, not one sin will be forgotten. The wages
of sin is *eternal death*, which means being separated from God, and this price
must be paid. But God, the Judge, laid aside his robes of glory and came to
us in Jesus; he paid that debt of sin once and for all when he died on the
cross. And now he comes to us by the Holy Spirit and asks us to receive him
into our hearts and start a new life with him, forgiven and joyful.

Scripture

He died for all, so that those who live should no longer live for themselves, but only for him who died and was raised to life for their sake. . . .
When anyone is joined to Christ, he is a new being; the old is gone,
the new has come. 2 Corinthians 5:15, 17

Prayer

Thank you, Lord, that you paid my debt by dying at Calvary.

Thank you that you came back from the dead to offer me a new start
in life. You have given me your Holy Spirit so that my life may be useful,
worthwhile, and purposeful. So help me, day by day, to turn away from
the things that spoil my life, and teach me to live close to you and to
work for you. Thank you, Lord, for this wonderful second start.

Have you personally experienced this new beginning in your life? If you have, in what ways are you trusting the Holy Spirit to help you make a fresh start?

Chapter 20

The Holy Spirit
reproduces Christ's life
in us

Colossians 3:1-4

THE MESSENGER

It was a beautiful spot in a remote valley in Brazil where Harry and Margaret lived with their two babies. Harry was a teacher in the newly formed rural Bible school, and they lived in a little home that they privately called "The House of a Thousand Fleas." The last owner had kept pigs under the floor, and they frequently had rat visitors. But they were very happy and warmly welcomed by their Brazilian neighbors. The two babies toddled about in the sunshine and became almost as brown as their small friends.

Not far from Harry and Margaret's home was a deep ravine spanned by a rather precarious wooden bridge. At the bottom, the river ran from east to west between the steeply rising banks. The southern bank, sloping down from cultivated fields, was a garden of beauty in spring. The sun shone on it all day long, and the deep roots of the plants bored down toward the water. A riot of glorious flowers cascaded down, and the butterflies swarmed above them.

But the northern bank was quite different. Bordering the jungle, it received no sun, and its soil was drained by the roots of great trees. Nothing grew except slimy fungi—just roots and earth and the cold smell of decay.

Early one morning, Harry left home mounted on his mule. Riding into town he watched the sunlight creeping down the mountains, chasing the shadows. He heard an ovenbird calling to its mate across the valley, and he saw a praying mantis standing on a low rock as if praising God for such a morning. Already the women were down at the river washing their clothes, and young white goats were skipping in the pastures.

It was when he was halfway across the bridge that Harry noticed the miracle—close to the bridge post on the north bank, where the sun never shone, grew a perfect white flower. It gleamed like a pure white star, alone among the rough roots and dark fungi. Harry crossed and reined his mule to a branch, then scrambled down the bank to investigate.

He was no botanist, but he thought it must be a kind of clematis. He lifted the bloom gently, and it came away from the earth at once. It had no root, only a frail tendril that twined round the post and clung to the boards on the lower side of the bridge. Such a frail tendril, so easily snapped, but it was doing its work. Over on the other side where the flowers bloomed and the birds sang and the sun shone, was the living root of the parent plant, pouring its sap into the tendril, reproducing its life in a cold, alien climate.

If that flower could have spoken, it would have said this: "I have no power of my own to bloom in this cold, dark soil, but my life is linked with a life that blooms over there in the Land of Sunshine. I am part of the parent root; my flowers are like the flowers that bloom yonder. I have brought all the beauty of that life over into this sad, dead place. I am a messenger from that land."

Although we may have to live in this world tarnished by sin, we do not have to blend in with our surroundings. The Holy Spirit has brought the very life of God into our hearts and linked us with Jesus. As this new life grows in us and we obey the voice of the Spirit in our hearts and in the Bible, we shall become like Jesus. Then those around us will see the love and truth and courage of Jesus shining out in the dark places of the earth.

Scripture

[Jesus said,] "Because I live, you also will live." John 14:19

Your life is hidden with Christ in God. Colossians 3:3

Prayer

Thank you, Lord, that the Holy Spirit lives in my heart. Now I am truly sharing your life, linked with you. I pray that today I may show out the life of Jesus—his love and kindness instead of my selfishness; his purity instead of the corruption of sin; and his truth in the place of dishonesty and lies. Fill me with your Holy Spirit that Jesus may live again in me, in the place where I am today.

Reflection

The tendril was the life line to the clematis. In your life have you seen how prayer is the life line for your relationship with God? What steps can you take to increase your hold on the life line of prayer?

Chapter 21

A HOME FOR VIRGINIA

*The Holy Spirit's power
transforms us*

*Romans 8:1-11;
2 Corinthians 3:18*

Awhile ago, the settlements where miners lived consisted of broken-down shacks and taverns. They were places where every man carried a knife and where many of the men were desperate characters who had good reasons for disappearing west with the digging gangs. Of all the settlements, however, Roaring Camp was the most notorious for drunkenness, murder, and general wickedness.

One wild night, a young girl on the point of collapse staggered into Roaring Camp and begged shelter. The nearest medical post was miles down the track, so no one really knew what to do. They laid her on a mattress in a deserted shack, and she closed her eyes and turned her face to the wall while they went in search of help. But when they came back, it was too late. The girl had died, leaving a wailing newborn daughter, but no clue of who she was, where she had come from, or where she was going.

After attending to her as best they could, the miners buried the girl in the soft earth down by the river. Now they had to decide what to do with the baby. Someone suggested putting the child on the next truck from the mine and sending it down to the nuns, but no truck was leaving for three days, and the baby was crying bitterly. The men were staring helplessly, when, to everyone's surprise, old Charlie strode through the middle of the group. He picked up the dirty, wailing little bundle.

"Leave her to me," he said abruptly. "I've reared a young 'un before now. You, Tom, find the shepherd on the hill over yonder, and tell him to bring some milk mighty quick, and you, Jo, go down to the trading store and don't come back without a baby's bottle."

The men were amazed. Charlie was probably the oldest man in the camp, and his shack was, if anything, the dirtiest. Lonely, grizzled, and despondent, he seldom joined in the wild behavior of the younger men. He would sit for hours staring out over the scarred landscape, chewing on his pipe. He seldom spoke, and no one knew where he had come from or what he was fleeing from. He was a strange, remote character, old Charlie, and no one cared to cross him.

Charlie carried the tiny girl home and laid her on his dirty blanket. He stood for a while gazing at her helplessly. He had had a baby daughter long ago, but his wife had left him and taken the child with her. He had not been sorry when his wife left, for they had learned to hate each other, but when little Virginia disappeared, something in him had died. "I'll call this little one Virginia," he murmured. "But my Virginia was clean as a white flower. Maybe I'd better wash this little one."

With the aid of some firewood, a tinderbox, a bucket, and some lye soap, the new Virginia was washed clean. It did seem a pity, though, to wrap a clean child in such a dirty blanket. Well, he had one clean linen shirt and a clean bit of toweling packed down somewhere at the bottom of his box. Charlie wrapped her in these and walked up and down with her, trying to quiet her hungry cries, till finally the shepherd arrived with some ewe's milk. It would take many hours to procure a bottle, so he tore off a strip of toweling, dipped it in the milk, and let the baby suck it. She soon fell asleep, peaceful and satisfied.

"She needs a cradle," Charlie muttered, resting his cheek on her down head. He knew he was beginning to become attached to her. Laying her down gingerly on the blanket, he went off to consult with the tavern keeper, who produced an empty packing case and some straw. The trading store eventually came up with a bottle, some baby clothes, a blanket, and plenty of white rags, and the shepherd agreed to come every day with milk. The whole settlement was getting interested now; old Charlie's brat was becoming their mascot.

A few days later Charlie stood looking down at his new daughter. Asleep, she was like a fair flower under her new clean blanket, with the white rags draped round the packing case. But something looked wrong—for the first time he noticed the filthy stains on the floor of his shack, contrasting harshly with the spotless cradle. He gave the boards a thorough scrubbing, and they finished up quite a different color. "Now your cradle will look just fine," he said triumphantly, lifting it back from the bed to the floor.

But now the floor looked all wrong and out of place. He had never before noticed the clinging dirt and vermin on the walls, and the black, smoke-grimed ceiling. *I'd best feed her and park her at Tom's,* he thought. *Then I can get down to the store for a brush and whitewash. I need summat to kill the vermin.*

Charlie worked hard for two days, and one or two of his mates helped him while another minded Virginia, the innocent cause of all the disturbance. On the second evening he carried her proudly back to her rejuvenated home and held her on his knee. She seemed to stare round at the white walls and ceiling with her solemn, baby blue eyes, and then she stared unwinkingly at Charlie—at his earth-and-tobacco-stained clothes, his ragged beard, his matted hair, and his great dirty hands. He began to feel uneasy. In fact, he felt rather uncomfortable in all this cleanness.

"Maybe I need to look in a mirror," he mused, but he possessed no such thing. He laid Virginia down and plodded off to the creek. Stooping forward, he gazed into the clear depths of a pool and chuckled. "Kinda need sprucing up," he muttered.

The barber trimmed his hair and beard, and Charlie bought new clothes at the store. He washed out his old ones and laid them aside for digging in the mine. He could not dig at present because he was too busy, so he was glad for his little hoard of gold buried down under the loose floorboard.

Little Virginia thrived in her palace, kept scrupulously clean by her adopted father. As spring gave place to summer and the weather grew warmer, he would carry her cradle out into the sunshine, where she would kick and crow and smile up at the sky and the flying birds.

But she'll soon be sitting up, thought Charlie. *And what'll she be a-looking at, with those baby blue eyes of hers a-staring? Trampled dirt and weeds, and an old trash heap! T'won't do!*

So Charlie started digging on his own patch of yard, and the store produced some flower seeds. He went to the forest and cut stakes to erect a fence, while his baby crowed approval and gurgled. In the early summer sunshine and sweet mountain air, his seeds grew fast, and, by the time Virginia's curly head was peering over the top of the cradle, his garden was a place of greenness and beauty.

Soon other rough men saw the transformation and caught the idea. Gradually other little gardens sprang up; other shacks were cleaned and whitewashed. "No reason for us all to live like hogs, is there?" asked the men.

No reason at all. And the reason for the change, of course, was the tiny new life of a baby washed clean in a bucket of water.

———◆◆◆◆◆———

When the Holy Spirit enters your heart, he creates a new, clean life within you. You can neglect it, or you can concentrate on it. Old Charlie made the new little life of Virginia central in his home. Everything else had to conform to it, and what did not fit had to be changed. For us, this means placing Christ in the center, showing up what is wrong, giving us the power to change, and transforming our lives with his beauty and love.

Scripture

Set apart to become like his Son. Romans 8:29

Prayer

O Lord, I pray that this new life that you have given me may be central, the most important thing of all. I pray that through constantly looking at Jesus I may see the things in me that need to be changed, the things that are ugly and sinful. I pray that his Holy Spirit may so fill me that because of that newborn life in me my whole person may be transformed.

Think of something that is wrong in your life, something that the Holy Spirit has laid on your conscience recently. Are you using his power to put it right?

Chapter 22

The Holy Spirit helps us see and reflect the image of Christ

2 Corinthians 4:1-6; 1 John 3:1-3

THE DEFACED LIKENESS

Young Sir Hugh was the first to see them coming. He was leaning on the gate, feeling miserable, as usual, when he suddenly looked up and recognized the cropped heads and sober attire of Cromwell's soldiers, who were galloping between the young green wheat acres that surrounded his home. It was April of the year 1649.

This story begins, however, in January. Sir Hugh's life received a crushing blow on that cold winter day when a horse came thundering up to the door, steaming with sweat, and the rider flung himself from the saddle, crying out the terrible news: King Charles had been executed at Whitehall, his son, Charles II, was in hiding, and their cause was lost. Cromwell's parliamentary forces were in power.

There was a great deal more news that day, but Hugh, who was thirteen years old, did not stay to hear it. He ran out into the garden, threw himself down under the wintersweet bush, and wept and wept. When at last he wiped away his tears, he noticed that the first snowdrops had pierced the oak mold. Perhaps all was not over. Perhaps, one day, there could be a new beginning?

Hugh began to daydream about the young prince in hiding. He often rode miles over the winter countryside, peering at every young man he met, just in case; for it was rumored that Charles II was hiding somewhere in the West Country. So obsessed did Hugh become with the idea of the outcast prince seeking shelter in his own family's manor that he gave little heed to studying his Greek and Latin, and his tutor was in despair. His father scolded him most sharply and threatened to cane him, but Hugh, after listening politely to all that his father had to say, burst out eagerly: "Good Sir, should we not get the attic prepared in readiness, lest His Majesty King Charles II should seek shelter here?"

The father's stern expression suddenly became sad and gentle. He understood now why his loyal young son could no longer keep his mind on his lessons. "My son," he said gravely, "may God preserve the prince and lead him to safety, but may God also preserve us from any such visitation. Would you want us all to follow our king to the scaffold? Are we not well known as loyalist supporters? Forget this thought quickly, child, and concentrate again on your studies."

Hugh said no more. And his father changed. He cropped his locks and laid aside his fine clothing and made Hugh do the same. They were now dressed as sober gentlemen farmers, and no one could tell for what party they stood. Nor did they talk about the kingdom any longer.

The boy, however, could not forget the prince he honored. He arranged his own little bedchamber with meticulous care, keeping an extra pile of clean bed linen from the linen closet always at hand. On the wall before the bed he hung the small portrait of Charles I that his father had purchased on his last visit to court—an exquisite likeness after the fashion of the Van Dyck paintings. If the prince came, he would be glad to look on that.

The prince never came. Then, on that April day, a company of Cromwell's stern Roundhead soldiers came cantering through the bright countryside, making straight for Hugh's home.

Hugh slid from the gate and ran up the drive. He had very little time, for the riders had seen him and were galloping after him. He could hear the thudding of horses' hoofs on the path, and he shot inside the front door just as they drew up. But they still had to dismount, so he reached his father alone.

"Good Sir, my father," he gasped, "they have come . . . the tyrant's men . . . they will search the house and question you as they did Squire Robinson."

"Then bid your mother hide the crested silver and all our Royalist clothing," replied his father. "Help her to cover all trace, while I detain them in the parlor."

Hugh reached his own little room only a few paces ahead of the search party. Already their boots were thumping on the stairs when he remembered—the picture on the wall! It was too late to hide it, and there was nowhere safe to put it. His father's voice drummed in his brain: "Would you want us to follow him to the scaffold?" He looked round wildly.

On his desk were a brush and painter's palette and a half-finished landscape, for Hugh was a young artist. He seized the brush and daubed green paint on the king's face—a rough apple—blotches of purple on the beautiful jeweled tunic—a few plums—and a smear of yellow for a plate under the whole. Then Sir Hugh stood boldly in front of the painting, legs apart, guarding his king, when the soldiers entered the room.

The Roundheads found nothing incriminating. After they left, Hugh gave the picture to his father, who hid it away in a cupboard, and there it stayed, forgotten and undisturbed for many years. Sir Hugh grew to manhood and welcomed his prince back to the throne of England. He served the king faithfully for many years, and when he died, his sons and their descendants lived on at the manor.

Nearly three centuries later, one of Hugh's descendants, an art lover, made the long hall into a picture gallery. And the little portrait hidden by those ugly daubs of paint was brought out to the light. The heir to the manor was puzzled. It seemed such a poor, insignificant painting, but it was obviously old, and the frame was beautiful, so it seemed worth keeping. He hung it high up in a rather dark corner and lost interest in it.

Then one day an eminent art dealer came down to see the collection. The two men passed through the gallery together, stopping here and there, examining, discussing prices. The western sun shone through the window, and a bright beam illuminated the strange little picture in the corner. The art dealer stopped short, peered intently, climbed on a chair to look closer, and then spoke in a voice of suppressed excitement. "Might I take down this small picture and examine it?" he asked.

"With pleasure," answered the owner. "I believe it has been in the family for years. It's mid–seventeenth century, but I've never discovered its history or what it's meant to be."

"Have I your permission to take it and investigate?" asked the dealer.

Permission was readily given, and late that night the dealer sat down to discover the mystery of the picture. He knew that those daubs of green and purple and yellow had never been applied by the hand that had painted that rich, shadowed background. With palette knife and chemicals he peeled off the outer layers, and there, clear and lifelike as on the day it was tinted, shone out the features of King Charles.

When we receive Christ's Holy Spirit into our hearts, our bodies become the temples of the Holy Spirit. The life and love of Jesus should therefore shine out with increasing brightness. But there are outward things that sometimes hide his glory and beauty, so that people cannot recognize Jesus living in us— carelessness, rudeness, selfishness, impatience. Anything that hides the character of Jesus matters to a Christian.

Scripture

The God who said, "Out of darkness the light shall shine!" is the same God who made his light shine in our hearts, to bring us the knowledge of God's glory shining in the face of Christ. 2 Corinthians 4:6

Prayer

"Grant me the beauty of the inner man, and may the outer and the inner be at one."—based on a prayer of Socrates

"Let the beauty of Jesus be seen in me
All his wondrous compassion and purity.

Oh thou Spirit divine,
All my nature refine,
Till the beauty of Jesus be seen in me."—unknown

Reflection

In your own life, what wrong things do you find particularly difficult to overcome? Make a point of asking God daily for help with those, trusting him as the God of the impossible.

Chapter 23

The Spirit produces love

Galatians 5

A SURPRISE FOR THE BRIGAND CHIEF

Chang was a Chinese brigand chief in the days when foreigners could enter China quite freely. He headed a notorious band of men who lived in hide-outs in the rocks, high up in the mountains where the government troops could never find them. On dark, windy nights they would creep out fully armed to the boundaries of villages. At a given signal, they would all rush in at once, first shooting down the fierce village dogs, then grabbing and looting and shooting anyone who tried to resist them. They would sell the loot, little by little, in far markets and only attack again when they came to the end of their profits. No village in the huge mountain district ever felt safe, for no one had ever managed to overcome the brigands or track them down.

Now a bigger scheme was afoot. Chang discussed the idea with his gang far up in the fastnesses of the rocks. They were an evil crowd, and nearly all hated and feared their leader, who always took the biggest share of the spoils. At the same time, most of them were fugitives from prison or death sentences and dared not return to their old haunts, so they listened sullenly while Chang spoke.

He told them that since the villages had yielded little loot recently, they needed to be more ambitious. Down to the south at the foot of the hills was a little town. There were shops and riches to be grabbed in that little town, and best of all there was a small clinic run by three foreign devils. People came from all over the district to get medicine at that clinic, and there were even a few beds for the very ill. The doctors, no doubt, were rich. There would be money in the hospital as well as blankets and all sorts of paraphernalia used by foreign devils. They would get a great haul from that town.

The men listened sulkily. It was a much more risky project than any they had attempted before, but to rebel against their leader in this meant certain instant death. To attack at least meant only probable death. They lived continuously on the fringe of death, but they knew of no other way to live. Those blankets Chang had mentioned would certainly be welcome in the cold mountain winter—if they were allowed to keep them.

The attack was planned for the dark night of the new moon. A scout had already been in to the market and made a plan of the lay of the land. The men gathered round the rough charcoal sketch, and everyone was told exactly what to do. The raid would only take a few minutes, beginning at the blast of Chang's whistle. Chang himself, with two of the band, was to attack the hospital.

When the night came, the brigands attacked, and at first all seemed to go according to plan. The night watchman at the hospital was quickly overpowered, and Chang and his two companions burst into the quiet little ward, grabbing and looting, dazzling the eyes of the startled orderly with a bright lantern. Just as they left, the foreign doctor came running out of the house with two foreign women behind him. They too were quickly dispatched: Chang brought the flat of his sword down with such a blow on the doctor's outstretched arm that he could hear the bone crack, and the unarmed women shrank back at the glitter of the knife blade. Only as Chang put his lips to the whistle did he realize that something was wrong: the town had been ready for them this time; the militia was installed.

A great battle went on, with shooting and screaming and terrified flying forms. Chang hesitated. He could pitch in and fight for his men, or he could drop his loot and disappear into the darkness of the forest behind the hospital. He decided that this must be a case of every man for himself. He made off into the forest, flinging his lantern down at the base of the timber walls, for the excitement of a fire would cover his retreat.

Cursing, stumbling, bruised, he pushed on over heaps of rubbish, falling into foul ditches and struggling through thorny bushes, until the screams and clash of arms grew faint and the blaze of fire made a red glow in the sky. Then he realized that he was alone with the night and the silence of the hills. Alone, but not safe! At dawn the militia would be patrolling the hills; he must get back to the mountain recesses, the caves and rocks and deep valleys. Sunrise found him lying exhausted in the shelter of the thickly wooded foothills—a terrified fugitive running for his life.

Chang was not caught. For days he journeyed on, crossing the mountains, begging in the villages, and sometimes helping in the harvests. No one suspected that this weary, footsore tramp was Chang, the robber king, the terror of the countryside.

Yet he could not rest. Evil and selfish as he was, he had been the head of a band of men. He had tyrannized them and cheated them, but now in his loneliness he longed for them. There had been no love between them, but in a strange way he had been proud of them. How many had died in that battle? How many had been taken by the militia? How many, besides himself, had escaped?

At last Chang could bear it no longer. The search must have been given up long ago, and even his own men would never recognize him now, shaved and dressed as he was, like a poor coolie. He decided to go down to the town and make inquiries. There in the plains he would seek employment, and perhaps in time he could purchase a little farm and a rice field. Love of fighting seemed to have died in him with the death of his gang. If there was any way of peace he would seek for it.

He entered the town with the stream of villagers on a bright market day and strolled round noticing everything without appearing to look at anything. The hospital had not been rebuilt yet, and the foreign devils were not there. He stood surveying the ruins and began to question a local inhabitant. "This is a pity. I hear it was a foreign house. How was it burned down?"

"The cursed robbers came. They burned the dispensary and wounded our doctor. Now he is gone. But they will surely return and rebuild."

"And what befell the cursed robbers? Were they slain, as they deserved?"

"Many were slain; some were taken. Three were wounded and lay dying."

"And what happened to those wounded dogs?"

"The militia would have dragged them away dying, but the doctor came out and pleaded for them. He said, 'Let them die here.'"

"He pleaded for them? Why? Did he want to kill them himself?"

"Oh, no! Those foreigners preach a religion of love. The hospital was burned down, so he took them into his house. His arm was broken, and he could not do much himself, but he told the women what to do. He went to another town where they put his arm in a plaster, but he was back next day. Night and day he watched over those three villains and cared for them as for his children. Those lions became lambs. One died, but two lived."

"And where are they now? Did he hand them over to the militia?"

"Oh, no. The militia counted them as dead and did not come back. When the doctor went away, those two went with him. They seemed like his sons. I do not think they will ever leave him."

Chang would not believe it. Only when he had heard this incredible story over and over again did it begin to dawn on him that he was hearing the truth. A man had loved his enemies—he had done good to those who had attacked and robbed and burned—and the enemies had become his friends. Love had proved stronger than the sword.

How could this be? This was no earthly love, born in the heart of men. That night, lying sleepless in the inn, Chang determined to search for the source of this love. The townsfolk had said that it was a religion of love, and there were others who held this religion.

He kept his resolve. Working at odd jobs and wandering from town to town, he sought for the religion that made a man love his enemies. And there came a day, finally, when Chang found followers of Jesus and learned at last about the source of that amazing love.

We see in Scripture that the source of forgiving love is God and that he sent that love streaming out to the world through Jesus. That same love is given to us through the Holy Spirit, so that we can learn to love and forgive as God does.

To know how God loved, read 1 John 4:7-21. To see how important this love is, read 1 Corinthians 13.

For God has poured out his love into our hearts by means of the Holy Spirit, who is God's gift to us. Romans 5:5

Prayer

"Love never fails,
Love is pure gold,
Love is what Jesus
Came to unfold.
Make us more loving,
Master, we pray,
Help us remember,
Love is your way."—unknown

Reflection

Jesus expressed God's principle of forgiveness perfectly in the Lord's Prayer: "Forgive us our sins as we forgive those who sin against us." How can you put this into practice?

Chapter 24

A SONG OF VICTORY

The Spirit produces joy

John 16:20-33

No one really knows exactly why Emperor Nero hated the early Christians in Rome so much. He had absolute power over the life and death of his subjects, and they lived in terror of him. The Christians, however, did not live in terror of him, for they had lost their fear of death. They knew that death itself could not separate them from the love of God; to them, dying meant making a joyful entrance into the presence of Christ. Many Christians even sang as they were being killed. Nero could kill their bodies, but he could not break their spirits. Perhaps this was one of the reasons why he hated them.

All through one summer Nero had enjoyed sitting in the Colosseum, the greatest open-air theater ever built, entertaining himself and the populace of Rome by watching Christians being thrown to wild beasts. But once the Roman winter came, the Colosseum was closed. What was to be done now, Nero wondered, with a band of forty Christian citizens who had been arrested and were awaiting the emperor's pleasure?

"Let them freeze!" snarled Nero, looking out on the winter landscape. He sent for a captain in his household guard to lead the forty prisoners to a small frozen lake in the hills above the city. There the prisoners were to be stripped and sent out onto the ice in the dark night to either recant or freeze to death. The captain and his men were to light a huge fire on the bank and remain beside it until the last condemned traitor had either fallen or walked back to the fire, denying his faith.

These were Nero's orders, so forty men stood together in the center of the frozen lake under the moonlit winter sky. Now and again, above the crackling of the fire and the sizzling of the soldier's roasted meat, a cry went up to the tingling stars—

> "Forty wrestlers wrestling for you, O Christ,
> Winning for you the victory, claiming for you the crown!"

The captain listened in sorrowful silence, for he too knew the Way of Christ. He believed that this Way led to everlasting life, but he had never dared to confess it. He had seen too many suffer; how could he endure what they faced?

Then suddenly everyone fell silent and all faces were turned to the lake; one stumbling figure was coming toward them, his head bowed in shame. The fierce pain of the cold and the sight of that fire had proved too much for his endurance, and he denied his faith. The soldiers burst into mocking laughter, dragged him ashore, clothed him, fed him, and inwardly despised him.

But out on the ice the song of triumph faded. The group stood in heartbroken silence. There was no more singing.

Then, once again, the laughter round the fire ceased, and the jesting group was struck dumb in astonishment. For they saw their captain rising, flinging away his warm clothing, and striding out, pale-faced and steadfast, onto the ice. There the group of believers welcomed him with rejoicing, and once again, though from voices ever weaker, the song ascended to heaven—

> "Forty wrestlers wrestling for you, O Christ,
> Winning for you the victory, claiming for you the crown!"

Scripture

You will show me the path that leads to life; your presence fills me with joy. Psalm 16:11

Prayer

O Lord, I pray that whatever happens to me in life, I may remember that you are the real source of my joy and that if I know and love you, I can rest in Jesus in spite of sadness or pain. Save me from grumbling, self-pity, or pessimism, and let me show those whom I meet that a Christian is a person with hope.

"Grant us, O Lord, the royalty of inward happiness and the serenity that comes from living close to you. Daily renew in us the sense of joy and let your eternal Spirit dwell in our souls and bodies, filling us with light and gladness, so that we may meet all that comes, even death itself, with courage and peace, always giving you thanks in all things. Amen."
—unknown

Reflection

How much does your gratitude to God depend on your ups and downs? With the help that God gives, practice *always* rejoicing in the Lord.

Chapter 25

The Spirit produces peace

John 14:27

THE WINNING ENTRY

The art-class students were having a discussion on the playground. Their exams were due at the end of term, and each had to submit a painting. They had been given a choice of subjects, and one of them was *Peace.*

"Quite a lot of scope for ideas there," commented one student. "A good seascape . . . an early morning scene . . . a sunset . . ."

"Oh, but that's not very original!" said another. "A night scene would be better, but night scenes are awfully difficult."

"What about an old man surveying the fruits of his years of labor? Oh, getting the expression on his face right would take more skill than I have. That wouldn't do either!"

"An animal study maybe. A cat curled up in the sunshine, but how do you draw a purr?"

"You could make it abstract—just a blending of colors."

"Well, there may be endless possibilities, but all the same, I think I shall choose another subject!"

After the deadline, the examiner briefly sorted the entries into their subjects. A number of students had attempted the subject *Peace,* and he was rather bored with their efforts. The stiff figure stretched out sunbathing on the beach looked as though her joints were immovable. The sunset sky was overdone; no one ever saw colors as lurid as that!

The examiner sighed, turned over another painting, and then suddenly stopped. Had he made a mistake? Could this wild, tossing seascape be entitled *Peace?*

He looked again. Then he understood.

The young artist had painted a storm at sea. She had achieved the impression of scudding clouds and curling green billows breaking in foam over a pitching ship in the foreground. At the back of the ship crouched a few roughly sketched figures. . . . Yes, this girl could draw. The attitudes portrayed terror, and some of the faces were lifted despairingly to the sky as though watching for some break in the storm.

In the stern of the ship, though, right in the forefront of the picture, stood a large figure drawn in greater detail—a man braced against a cabin door, somewhat sheltered from the wind, looking down at the child he held so tight against his shoulder. And in the child's small lifted face there was neither fear nor distress. The storm might rage around him, but he was asleep in his father's arms.

———◆·►◄·■———

The peace that the world gives depends on clear skies, safe surroundings, freedom from conflict, disturbance, and worry. But the peace that Jesus gives lasts right through the storms. Nothing can touch us or hurt us without God allowing it to happen and bringing us benefit through it. To know and trust that he is in control, whatever our situation, is to know peace.

Scripture

[Just before he died, Jesus said to his disciples,] "Peace is what I leave with you; it is my own peace that I give you. I do not give it as the world does. Do not be worried and upset; do not be afraid." John 14:27

Prayer

"Drop your still dews of quietness,
Till all our strivings cease,
Take from our souls the strain and stress,
And let our ordered lives confess
The beauty of your Peace."—John Whittier

Reflection

Think of a time when you have felt peace from God. Was it during happy circumstances or during difficult ones? How can you remind yourself to concentrate on the peace Jesus gives in every circumstance you face?

Growing in Faith

Just as a young plant needs a good environment of proper nourishment and water, sunshine and rain to grow in a healthy way, we also need spiritual food to grow as Christians. Here are a few areas we all must concentrate on as we seek to deepen our faith:

* *Listening to God's voice.* God does speak to us in a variety of ways, but one important way of hearing his voice is to read and think about the Bible.

* *Talking to God.* Prayer does not have to be dull in any way, nor should it be a shopping list of daily requests. Prayer can be instead a way of life as we live constantly in the awareness of God's presence, being open to him and talking with him throughout the day.

* *Serving God.* As believers we need to find out how we can serve God best, giving special thought to our personalities, the natural gifts and abilities God has given us, and the time and opportunities we have.

* *Meeting with other believers.* Joining a church, Sunday school, or youth group not only offers us opportunities for help and encouragement but also puts us in situations where we can help others.

* *Keeping a pure heart.* If we sin, we must ask forgiveness and put it right quickly, thus keeping a clear conscience.

* *Growing in faith.* When in difficulty, we need to look more and more to God's supreme power and his love for us, rather than focusing on the size of our problems.

Chapter 26

We listen to God's voice through Scripture

Psalm 11

THE BOOK IN THE BEDSIDE CUPBOARD

Moshe was a French-born Jew. All through his childhood he had been taken to the synagogue, Sabbath after Sabbath, where he heard the Old Testament read. His father was a wealthy businessman who was deeply religious and, like all other Orthodox Jews, awaited the coming of the promised Messiah. Moshe had never read of Jesus, who fulfilled all that was written in the Old Testament about the One who should come.

Moshe loved and honored his father, eagerly awaiting the day when he should become his partner in the firm. They often talked together, and one day they got onto the subject of religion. Moshe told his father of a classmate whom he particularly admired.

"He is the kindest, best boy that I know," said Moshe. "But he reads the New Testament and often talks about it. Dad, why is it so wrong to read the New Testament?"

Instantly his father became agitated. "My son," he said, "keep away from that book, for it tells a pack of lies. It tells that our Messiah has already come and that our nation failed to recognize him and crucified him. Moshe, I want you to promise me that you will never read that book."

Moshe considered his father's request. The mystery of the book intrigued him. "Never is a long time, Dad," he replied. "I will promise you this, though. I will not open the New Testament until I am twenty-one. After that, I feel I ought to judge for myself." And with that, his father had to be content.

Years passed, and at twenty years of age, Moshe was a trusted young man rising to a partnership in his father's firm. It was a proud day for him when his father sent him to England as the firm's representative to handle an important business deal. He had never been to England before, although he spoke English fluently along with three other languages. London thrilled him, and he intended to stay on for a few days to see the sights when his business was finished. Booked in a comfortable hotel, Moshe settled down in his room on the first evening to sort out his papers and prepare for his interviews.

But to his surprise, on opening his bedside cupboard, he found a Gideon

New Testament lying there! Moshe shut the cupboard quickly and tried to forget it, but somehow he found it hard to concentrate on his business. What was so dangerous and mysterious about the forbidden book? He longed to look, but there were still a few months to go before his twenty-first birthday, and his promise bound him. All through his business appointments and the excitement of sightseeing, the thought haunted him: *Why does my father hate and fear this book so? What makes it so dangerous and so alluring?*

On the last night of his visit, Moshe could stand it no longer. *My father had no right to bind me to this promise,* he said to himself. *I am twenty and a man. I will read the first chapter only, and then I will sleep.*

His fingers trembled a little as he opened at the first chapter of Matthew, but as he read he was surprised and disappointed—it was merely a genealogical tree, a list of Old Testament names that he knew already. There was nothing dangerous or mysterious about this. He read on boldly nearly to the end of the chapter. Here there was a short account of the birth of Christ. He read more slowly. At verse 21 he stopped with a shock after he read these words: "You will name him Jesus—because he will save his people from their sins."

Moshe read that verse again and again. He remembered nothing in his Jewish religion that told him a person could be saved from his sins. He longed to do right and to keep God's law, but he knew that from childhood onwards he had broken that law again and again, and he supposed he always would. Was there really someone who could save him from sinning? Could he be freed from that sense of guilt and become what he wanted to be? If so, he had found the answer to the biggest question in his life.

He shut the book, for he must not break his promise any further, but he could not sleep. He had to know more. Next morning he traveled home, his business successfully accomplished, but somehow his father's proud congratulations failed to please him as much as he had expected. Only later on, when the celebrations of his homecoming were over, did Moshe blurt out, "Father, I have broken my promise. I read the Book."

Moshe then had to face a most difficult time. His father made it clear from the first that he must make a choice. If he decided to become a Christian, he would no longer be allowed to become a partner or even to remain employed in his father's firm.

Moshe waited until he was twenty-one; then, with a clear conscience, he started to study the Book for hours on end. Through it God spoke to him, and he recognized Christ as the Messiah of the Old Testament, the Son of God, his Savior, and the One to whom he owed everything. He left home and started to preach the gospel to his own people, the Jews.

I do not know the end of the story, or whether Moshe was ever received back into his family. When I met him he was suffering loneliness and persecution, but deep down in his heart he was a joyful man. For through the Book he had found the real answer to life: he had found Jesus.

Scripture

Your word is a lamp to guide me and a light for my path. Psalm 119:105

Prayer

Open my eyes, so that I may see the wonderful truths in your law. Psalm 119:18

Reflection

To read the Bible carefully, with the willingness to learn from it and obey it, is a most certain way of hearing God's voice. From Scripture you can also learn much about the character of God. This in turn can help encourage you to communicate with him more in your daily life.

THE WHITE BIRDS

Chapter 27

When we pray sincerely, we listen and speak to God

Psalm 66:18

I once read about someone who had a very strange dream. He dreamed that an angel beckoned him to follow and led him into a church where five people were kneeling in prayer. In front of each person sat a white bird with folded wings. "Watch these people at prayer," said the angel, "and mark what happens to the white birds."

So the dreamer watched the first person. She was a woman, beautifully dressed, kneeling right in the front of the church. She prayed with her face lifted and the words flowing from her lips. Her white bird was the largest and finest and whitest of them all, but although she prayed and prayed, it never moved nor even fluttered a feather.

"Put out your hand and touch it," said the angel.

The dreamer gently touched the perfect white feathers and drew back his hand hastily. "I believe it's dead," he murmured.

"Yes," replied the angel sadly. "It's quite dead. This woman has been to church since childhood. She puts on her best clothes, and she knows all the best prayers by heart. Her words are beautiful, but she does not mean them, and when she leaves the church she forgets all about them. While she is praying, she does not even think about what she is saying. Look! She is glancing at her neighbor in the next pew and wondering how much her hat cost."

The dreamer moved to the second kneeling figure. He seemed to be praying well. The beautiful white bird in front of him stirred its feathers and soared upwards, and the dreamer, following its flight, noticed that the church had no roof. Up the bird mounted, straight into the blue. Then, suddenly, the face of the praying man changed. His devout expression became hard and bitter, and he pressed his lips together, muttering something under his breath. The beautiful, soaring bird dropped as though an arrow had pierced it and lay dead on the church floor. The dreamer turned questioningly to the angel.

"That man started to pray sincerely," said the angel. "As he prayed, however, he remembered someone who had wronged him. Anger flooded his heart, and he turned from love. He will not forget, and he will not forgive. See, he is hurrying out to plan some revenge, so his prayer never reached the Father."

The dreamer paused before the third praying figure. A woman was kneeling, her hands clasped, the marks of tears on her cheeks. As she prayed, the fair white bird in front of her began to rise and then sank again. It summoned its strength and rose again, reached almost to the top of the pillar, and then seemed to fall. But before it reached the ground, it struggled up again, beating its wings, and at last it reached the clear blue air, fluffed out its feathers, and disappeared into the sunshine.

The angel, who had been watching anxiously, drew a sigh of relief, saying, "This woman has passed through great sorrow. She could no longer believe that God loved her or cared for her. She had not been here for a long time, but today she came back and tried to pray. As she prayed, her doubts returned . . . she could not believe . . . she nearly gave up. But she told the Lord about her doubts and whispered the promises of God, and her faith was strengthened. Her prayer reached the Father, and he has drawn near to comfort her. See? She is smiling!"

The fourth kneeling figure seemed to be a tramp from the streets, and in front of him huddled a weak, dingy bird looking as though it could not rise at all. The man did not seem to be speaking; he just looked wretched. But, all of a sudden, the dull wings quivered, and the bird flew straight upwards in strong flight. As it reached the open sky, its wings, kissed by the sunshine, gleamed white as snow, and the angel laughed for joy.

"That man does not know how to pray at all," said the angel. "He has never prayed in his life and does not know what words to use. But his heart is heavy with his sin and need, and his thoughts are crying out for mercy and forgiveness. Just at this moment all the angels of God in heaven are rejoicing because another sinner has come home."

The last person in the church was a little boy, and in front of him sat a tiny, spotless bird. The child folded his hands and said that he was sorry that he had slapped his sister. He asked God to make his mother well and please to help him with his sums. He thanked God for the football he had had on his birthday, and the bird flew straight upwards with a song of joy. Then the child jumped up and ran out into the garden to kick his ball, laughing up into the face of the angel as he passed by.

There are as many ways of praying as there are people of prayer. It is neither the form of prayer, nor the place, nor the position—kneeling, standing, or walking—that really matters. The important thing to God is the inner attitude of your heart.

Scripture

If I had ignored my sins, the Lord would not have listened to me. Psalm 66:18

May my words and my thoughts be acceptable to you, O Lord, my refuge and my redeemer!—a prayer of David from Psalm 19:14

Reflection

When you know that your heart is not right with God, what do you usually do?

+ Feel guilty all over and shrivel up
+ Go out and enjoy myself to forget all about it
+ Just hope I will do better next time
+ Pretend to myself that it matters neither to God nor to me
+ Avoid facing God about it and put on a brave face
+ Tell God honestly all about it, about how I feel, and ask him to forgive me and help me start afresh

Which alternative do you think God wants you to choose?

Chapter 28

AISHA'S LETTER

*We pray in the name of
Jesus*

John 16:23-27

Old Aisha lived in a village high among the rocks looking out toward the Riff Mountains. She had lived in that village all her life, and except for an occasional trip to market, it was the only world she knew. As a child she had tended the goats high up where the charcoal burners lit their fires among the scrub. As a girl she had later married and traveled on horseback from one little thatched hut under the fig trees at the top of the village to another thatched hut by the well at the bottom of the village. Here she had ground corn and drawn water every day of her life, and here she had borne and brought up her children. But now her husband had died and the children had married and gone off to other villages, so old Aisha was left alone.

What troubled her most was that she seemed to be going blind, and whatever would happen to her then? Her daughters loved her, but her sons-in-law did not want her in their homes; besides, her own little home was dear to her. Perhaps something could be done about her eyesight. One night when her neighbors came back from market, she tackled them on the subject.

They were quite encouraging. Yes, there was a missionary nurse in the little market town, and she had good medicine. Many went there and were cured of coughs and spots and sore eyes, and no, she did not ask for money. Yes, old Aisha should certainly go, and they would take her with them on the mule when they next went in. Aisha went home comforted, sure that her sight would be restored.

A week later Aisha sat in the small mission dispensary, peering round and waiting her turn. When the time came, the nurse greeted her kindly, examined her eyes, and told her to sit down again. When all the other patients had gone, the nurse came and talked to her alone in her own language, an experience Aisha found so surprising that it was quite a long time before she found herself able to listen to anything that was said. But at last they found themselves communicating.

"I can't do anything for your eyes," said the nurse. "You need an operation. My brother in the town by the coast is an eye doctor. I think he could make you see."

"But how would I get to him?"

"In the bus."

"But I've never been in the long-distance buses, and I have no money."

"Perhaps your children would help you?"

"But if I went, what would I do when I got there? I've never been in the town, and I would get lost."

"You must ask your way to the hospital. Everyone knows the hospital."

"Even if I get there, the doctor might not let me in. I'm only a poor old woman, and he won't understand my language."

"He sees many poor old women every day, and he speaks your language. Besides, I will give you a letter telling him that you have come from far."

The idea of a letter seemed to comfort Aisha. She went back to the village and got in touch with her children. One day she arrived back at the dispensary with her son-in-law, who was going to buy her a ticket and put her on the bus. Then another distant relative would meet her in the town and lodge her. But, before anything else, she wanted that letter. Aisha had great faith in that letter; she finally left content with it in her hands.

It was quite a long time later that the nurse saw her again, and Aisha was hardly recognizable. The shuffling feet and the peering look had quite changed. She wore spectacles and walked confidently. She could see!

Aisha waited till all had gone from the dispensary for the day to tell her story. The nurse took her upstairs and, over a glass of mint tea, listened to her recount her experiences. Smiling, the listener imagined the scene: the busy outpatient department, the crowds at the door, the harassed doctor, and the determined old woman.

"I went up early in the morning, as you said," began Aisha. "And as I feared, I got lost. The relative with whom I stayed gave me money for the bus, but I got the wrong one, and it was already the time of the second prayer call when I arrived. The door was shut, and there were many standing outside, late like me, knocking at that shut door. Finally, the doorkeeper came out and told us that the room was full; we must all go away and come back in the afternoon, or next day. No one else could come in. The people argued and some were angry, but it was no use. The door had to be shut.

"Then I held up my letter, and I shouted in a loud voice, 'But I come in the name of his sister; I come in the name of his sister!'"

Aisha explained that the doorkeeper stopped and glanced at the letter. He thought it seemed authentic, and for all he knew, it might even be urgent. He admitted her and took her to the consulting room, where the doctor, recognizing the writing, read the letter immediately and took a look at her eyes. The condition was obvious to him, and he went about admitting her at once. It was all a perfectly ordinary, routine event, but to her it had seemed wonderful.

"The doorkeeper beckoned me in," Aisha exclaimed with shining eyes. "I alone! All the others had to go away. There were many waiting, but he led me through the crowds in front of them all into the presence of the doctor. And

I said again, 'I come in the name of your sister.' Many were waiting, but he turned from them and took the letter from me and read it right there. And then he turned to me, I who am old and poor, and he did for me all that you asked—a bed, an operation . . . and now I can see."

Aisha paused and considered. When she spoke again, her voice was soft and wondering. "How precious is your name to him," she murmured. "He did for me all that you asked. How precious is your name!"

<hr>

"In the name of Jesus" is not a magic formula to have our prayers answered. As we have seen, it is Jesus' life, death, and resurrection that have brought us back to God. It is because of what Jesus has done that we are again acceptable to God and can come to him through prayer. It is therefore by our faith in Jesus, because of our belief in him, that our prayers are heard. By praying "in Jesus' name," we are simply acknowledging to God, and reminding ourselves, that we owe our new relationship with God entirely to Jesus and his work. Praying this way also means that, just as the nurse asked for certain things for Aisha in her letter and signed it in her name, so we can ask and receive anything the Lord wants us to have, and this includes everything that he has promised us in the Bible.

Scripture

[Jesus] is able, now and always, to save those who come to God through him, because he lives forever to plead with God for them. Hebrews 7:25

[Jesus said,] "I am telling you the truth: the Father will give you whatever you ask of him in my name." John 16:23

Prayer

Father, thank you that I can be your child because of Jesus. Thank you also that I can come to you and ask for whatever I need. Help me never to forget what a miracle it is to be able to come to you in Jesus' name.

Reflection

Do you ever wonder if you are important enough or good enough or faithful enough for God to listen to? Make a habit of remembering that we never have to earn the right to talk with God—God listens and answers believers because of his Son, Jesus.

Chapter 29 THE RESCUE

We pray for others

Philippians 4:6-7;
Colossians 4:2

Mark woke up early one Saturday morning and knew that the summer had really come because the sunshine was so bright and the birdsong so urgent. He jumped out of bed and ran to the window. The world looked exactly as he had expected it to look, with fields sparkling silver and mists tangled in the willow trees along the stream banks. The buttercups would shortly be wide open, and there was no time to lose. Mark slipped on his clothes and tiptoed downstairs. He raised an eyebrow at the puppy, who flopped out of its basket and followed him. Then they skipped out into the waking, breathing garden. He was glad for a Saturday when he did not need to be back in time for school. And everyone slept later on Saturday, so he had plenty of time before breakfast.

By the gate Mark hesitated. With so many places to visit, it was hard to decide which to choose. He could climb the hill behind the house and chase the wild donkeys and look for larks' nests, or he could turn left into the bluebell woods and see if the hedge sparrow nestlings had flown yet. In the end he decided to follow the road down into the valley and make his way along the streambed to see how the frog spawn was getting on. The whole place should be hopping with baby frogs by now.

It was fun exploring along the stream bank under the tunnel of hazels, pushing through the cow parsley and sometimes using stepping stones, while the puppy scampered along in the grass just above him. Mark had nearly reached the frog pool when he suddenly stopped, almost tripping over what lay on the bank, half hidden by grass and nettles.

It was a fawn cow, and Mark had almost trodden on top of her. She had obviously slipped and hurt herself quite badly, for she lay very still, her head half in and half out of the water, her nostrils just above the surface. Staring down at her, Mark could hear her labored breathing and then, a moment later, a faint moo.

Well, she's still alive, anyhow, he thought. *I simply must get her out somehow. She'll drown if her head sinks any farther into the water.*

He climbed a little higher up the bank, took hold of her back legs, and began to pull, but the great animal was far too heavy for him. She switched her muddy tail against his shirt and let out a low moan. Mark slipped off his sandals, rolled up his trousers, and splashed into the stream. Perhaps he could lift her. He managed to raise the heavy head and rest it on a stone, but that was all. She rolled her eyes at him and struggled weakly.

It's no use, thought Mark sadly. *I'm only hurting her. I can't do anything. She's far too heavy. And I don't know what Mum will say about my clothes; they are covered with mud and sopping wet and all for nothing!*

He climbed up the bank again and emerged from the hazel trees into a buttercup meadow where other cows grazed. He picked up his puppy and looked round thoughtfully. *Cows belong to somebody,* he said to himself. *I can't see a house, but there must be a farmer somewhere. How silly of me to waste all that time. The farmer will know what to do if I can only find him.*

He climbed the golden slope, and, sure enough, just over the top was a rambling farmhouse, surrounded by barns. Smoke was rising from the chimney, and the farmer was eating bacon and eggs with his wife in the kitchen when Mark began his frantic banging on the back door.

The farmer opened the door to find a wet, dirty, excited little boy hopping from one leg to the other on his doorstep and a puppy barking in the background. "It's a cow," gasped Mark, who had been running very hard. "She's lying in the stream, and her head's nearly underwater. . . . Oh, please come quick! I tried so hard, but she's much too heavy."

The farmer swilled down his mug of tea. "Call Jim," he said to his wife. "I'm going to the barn for a rope. . . . You show us the way, son."

They were soon standing on the bank of the stream looking down at the poor creature. "Best bring her up on the grass and look at her there," said the farmer. "Fix the rope round her front legs, Jim, and I'll see to her back."

"Can I help?" asked Mark.

The farmer glanced at his hopeful face and smiled. "Why, yes," he said. "Seeing as you're so wet in any case, you might as well get down into the water and catch hold of her head." So Mark crouched in the stream, talking to the frightened cow and holding her head while the two strong men above him drew her gently up into the sunny meadow.

As Mark remembered his own hopeless little efforts, he chuckled. *To think that the farmer was there all the time,* he thought. *Why didn't I think to fetch him and tell him straight away?*

If we love the Lord and want to help other people, there are times when we really do not know what to do or how to help. But there is one thing that can never be wrong: we can always pray for those people and ask God to help them. He created them, he loves them, and he knows exactly what they need. When we commit a person to God, he draws near to that person in a new way.

Don't worry about anything, but in all your prayers ask God for what you need, always asking him with a thankful heart. Philippians 4:6

Prayer

Father, I pray for my family and friends and especially for _____ and _____, who need your help. Father, draw near to them and bless them and teach them more about your love. And show me too if there is anything I can do to help them.

Reflection

Your prayers, however insignificant you may think they are at times, do affect the lives of others. When you pray for people, do you remember that God loves them and cares for them far more than you do, and do you expect God to help them? Have you sometimes considered that you might be the helper God has chosen for the very person you are praying for?

WHAT MADE THE WALL FALL?

Lilias Trotter grew up in a large, wealthy family many years ago. While spending a holiday in Italy with her mother, she had been out sketching. Her mother, having heard that the famous art critic John Ruskin was staying in the same hotel, wrote him a note asking him to look at Lilias's drawings. He agreed rather unwillingly. He had always maintained that no woman could really paint. But what he saw made him change his mind.

Ruskin became Lilias's teacher and friend, convinced that the young woman was destined to become one of the greatest artists of the century. He did not understand that art was not her greatest love and so was bitterly disappointed when, as a young woman, she gave up painting as a career. Lilias went to Algeria in North Africa to work among Moslem women and founded what later came to be called the Algiers Mission Band.

The mission work was very hard work. Also difficult for someone who loved beauty so much was her life centered in the slums and alleys of a large town. But Lilias had the privilege of traveling, too. She loved the great spaces of the Sahara and often painted desert scenes. Over her bed hung a map of North Africa, and she would spend many hours kneeling in front of it, praying for the scattered towns and villages of Algeria.

Only very few people listened to Lilias give the message of the gospel, and sometimes she felt discouraged. Sometimes she was tempted to ask, *What is the good of praying? God does not seem to be answering, and so few are coming to believe in Christ.*

One day something happened, however, that taught Lilias to keep on praying, for prayer is never wasted.

She was sleeping in the house in the crowded alley very early one morning when suddenly, without the slightest warning, the wall between her house and the next fell in with a crash. Mercifully, Lilias was not hit, but her room was littered with dust and lath and plaster, and she found herself staring into the narrow passage that divided her home from the baker's shop next door. She could not understand why the wall had fallen, for she had seen no crack in the wall. Right away she sent for the local builder and asked him to rebuild the wall and also to try and discover the cause of the collapse.

The builder, who was also something of an architect, took a good look at the damage and then went for a stroll outside; he came back quite excited. "I have found the cause," he said. "I will tell you truly why your wall fell."

He explained that under the baker's shop was a sort of stone cellar with an oven and a seesaw-like machine for kneading the bread, which the baker set in motion every night. For over twenty years the machine had set up nightly vibrations, imperceptibly shaking her wall and gradually weakening it until that fateful early morning when the last vibration had done its work and the wall collapsed.

The builder rebuilt the wall, and the neighborhood was most sympathetic. Lilias did not regret the incident, however, for it had taught her something important—it had given her a picture of the strength of prayer. While she often had felt as if her prayers for the people of Algeria were wasted, she now saw they were each important steps in her work. Just as every vibration had weakened her wall, so every prayer prayed in the name of Jesus was weakening the stronghold of sin and suffering around her.

Lilias and others with her went on praying daily. They knew that one day, if they persevered and believed and endured, the fortress would fall.

Scripture

At all times carry faith as a shield; for with it you will be able to put out all the burning arrows shot by the Evil One. . . . Do all this in prayer, asking for God's help. Pray on every occasion, as the Spirit leads. For this reason keep alert and never give up; pray always for all God's people. Ephesians 6:16, 18

Prayer

Lord, you know that I often pray so long for something and nothing seems to happen. Help me to believe that every prayer prayed in your name is heard and achieves something and that in the end God's love and goodness will triumph over hate and sin. Keep me from giving up and becoming discouraged. Show me the things you want me to ask for, and then make me patient and steadfast and persevering in prayer.

Reflection

Why do you think God does not always answer prayer immediately? Although we may not realize it each time, God does in fact always answer prayer—but not necessarily in the way or at the time we expect.

Chapter 31

SEASIDE HOLIDAY

We pray knowing that
God loves to give

Matthew 7:7-11

I t was their very first visit to the seaside, and it was all very, very exciting. They even had a special song that their mother had made up for them, with a chorus:

> Little spades rattling,
> Buckets a-clattering,
> Off to the seaside are we!

The three eldest children, aged six, four, and three, started packing days and days before they were due to go, although they usually unpacked again every morning. Six and Four had a small, battered attaché case each, and Three had a little basket. The baby would have much more luggage than anyone else, but it would be packed for him.

When the children's mother found them enthusiastically packing most of the toy cupboard and bookcase, she made one rule. Each child could take one toy and one only, because, after all, they would be playing on the sand and in the sea, and they would not need toys. This caused some heart searching for Three, for all her dolls wanted to go to the sea, but no hesitation at all for Four, because he had already decided that he would just take Eskie. None of his toys really mattered compared with Eskie, for Eskie was part of the family. She had once been a handsome doll with a furry bundle of a baby on her back, but her earlier acquaintances would no longer have recognized her, for Eskie had had quite a life! She had traveled by post to Brazil and then back to England in her owner's arms. She had been chewed on and squashed into picnic baskets; she had fallen out of prams and been retrieved from the bath. She had long ago parted company with her baby and was now really nothing more than a gray lump of mangy-looking fur. Still, her faithful-hearted owner loved her just the same and never went anywhere without her.

The children thought the seaside at Woolacombe the most wonderful place in the world, and for their parents, too, the first week was a perfect holiday. The sun shone every day, and the children never tired of building sandcastles, exploring pools, and running in and out of the sea. Every day they wheeled the pram to the beach after breakfast, taking a picnic lunch, and returned somewhere near bedtime, sandy and gloriously happy.

Then, at the beginning of the second week, a sort of tragedy struck. It was the day that they made the Great Sandcastle. The tide was coming in fast; the children were making a big barrier, and their mother and father were helping. It was the most exciting thing they had ever done, for the waves were quite big and rough that day—large enough to knock over a tiny child if the water suddenly broke through the wall. The children squealed with delight at each fresh onslaught and piled on the sand. Nobody noticed how the water was creeping up on either side of the castle until the mother noticed the picnic basket about to set sail and ran to rescue it.

Of course the tide won the fight for the Great Sandcastle and the breathless, laughing children finally retreated, with Three riding on her father's back. It was only then that they realized that Eskie was missing. All during the holiday she had gone daily with the family to the beach, where she was usually propped in the picnic basket and left to admire the view. On this day, though, Eskie had sat in a little private sandcastle of her own. Now her little castle was covered with water, and the waves had carried her off.

Four was brokenhearted. His father swam round and round searching, but it was too rough to see the bottom, and, anyhow, Eskie could have been carried right out to sea. There was nothing to be done but to go back to their rooms. Four choked back his sobs, but he could hardly swallow his supper, and when the children collected for evening prayers just before bedtime, he whispered that they should pray for Eskie. So they lovingly committed Eskie to God and prayed that she would come back—after which Four seemed comforted and fell asleep.

Two days passed. Four was rather silent and spent much of his time on the beach searching pitifully up and down. His parents wondered how long his grief would last, and for three nights they prayed together, as a family, that Eskie would come back.

On the fourth morning, the usual procession started for the beach—Father, Mother, pram, baby, picnic basket, spades, buckets, and three little children prancing eagerly ahead. Suddenly they all turned and ran back, for a large dog had come bounding up the road, dripping with seawater and apparently making straight for them. Three clasped her daddy's trousers, and the other two got cautiously behind him.

On came the dog with huge leaps till he was close enough for Six to see that there was something in his mouth! The *something* was shapeless, gray, and sodden, but the mother suddenly darted forward and seized it. The dog let go and bounded on, and there was a moment's dazed silence, then cries of joy and laughter as the bedraggled Eskie was placed in Four's arms and his sad brown eyes lit up like stars.

And in case you say that this story is too good to be true, I can assure you that it really happened. For I was Three.

Scripture

In their trouble they called to the Lord, and he saved them from their distress. Psalm 107:6

Prayer

Thank you, Lord, for every prayer of mine to which you have said yes. Thank you for everything that I have asked for and you have given. Thank you for every time when I have cried to you in trouble or illness and you have helped me and healed me. Thank you that you care about even the little things and that you love to give me what I ask for.

Reflection

Try to remember three times when you asked God for something and he answered yes. Was your prayer answered in the way you expected? Have you thanked God for his answers?

Chapter 32

THE RAINBOW PULLOVER

S he stood at the door, one bare foot on top of the other, peering cautiously into the passage. Tied to her back, sleeping, was a tiny, dirty-faced sister. A slightly bigger child clung to her hand. Out in the street the mountain drizzle had soaked their ragged clothing, so they had come to school.

Mfuddla, Sodea, and Fatima lived in a hut with a flock of goats in a mountain village in North Africa. Their father had died, and every day their mother took the goats up into rocks where they could find grazing. Early in the morning she would sell the goat milk in the marketplace, give the children some bread, and then turn them out to beg in the streets. The hut was locked till she returned with the flock in the evening, unless it rained very hard. Then she would come back sooner.

When Mfuddla and Sodea heard that a school had been opened for children like them, they began to ask questions. What they heard seemed attractive: It was an odd sort of school. You turned up as soon as you had begged enough, but if you got there by ten, you got coffee, bread, and olives. You learned knitting and reading, and then the missionary in charge, who was also a nurse, told stories out of her book. And if you had spots or sore eyes or coughs (the sisters had all three between them), she gave you medicine. It sounded just right.

So Mfuddla, Sodea, and Fatima became regular schoolgirls, ones who always managed to arrive in time for breakfast. Mfuddla was very quick with her letters, and when Fatima cried on her back, she would walk up and down, rocking her to and fro, chanting her alphabet. What she liked best, though, was knitting. She was making a rainbow-colored pullover for Sodea from the scraps of bright wool that people sent from England. If she hurried, she might be able to make one for Fatima and one for herself before another winter came round.

Mfuddla always put her little sisters first, but otherwise she was rather selfish. If anyone took the ball of wool she wanted, she would stamp her bare foot, and her eyes would flash. She even tried to hide little balls of wool under cushions, but they were usually discovered.

The pullover grew in a glory of red, blue, white, and yellow stripes, and the thought of it brightened the shadowy little hut and the sacks that served the girls as blankets. But then, one Friday, the nurse made a terrible announcement: the wool supply was finished. They could come back on Monday for reading and Bible stories, but the knitting would have to wait.

"Till when?" asked Mfuddla sharply. The nurse did not know. There was no wool like that in the village, and to buy it in the town for such a crowd would be much too expensive. The wool they used came in occasional parcels from friends in other countries, and the nurse's brother brought any parcels up once a month by car. She was expecting him in a fortnight's time, but whether or not he would bring any wool she could not say. Mfuddla would just have to wait.

But Mfuddla had no intention of waiting. She sat considering. Suddenly she looked up and said slowly, "But you told us that Jesus Christ answers when we pray. So let us ask him to send us the wool by Monday."

The nurse hesitated; how could wool come by Monday? Parcels never came to the village. But she had no chance to say anything, for Mfuddla was already arranging the children and the empty suitcase where the wool was kept. They knelt round it in a ragged little crowd, faces lifted, hands cupped to receive, as they were used to doing when begging. Quite simply, Mfuddla told the Lord that they needed the wool to finish their pullovers and asked if he would be sure to send it by Monday morning. Then school proceeded as usual, except that the nurse felt troubled. How could wool possibly come by Monday morning?

Just before the children went home, there was a commotion in the street, a loud knocking at the door, and shouts of "Telephone! Telephone!" A rich merchant who lived at the corner of the market owned a telephone, and in an emergency he let the nurse use it. Now someone had called asking for her. It was always an exciting occasion when this happened. Those in the street would run along behind her and wait at the great studded door to hear the news. The household inside would crowd round as she talked and want every word relayed. That day it was her brother who was waiting at the other end of the line.

"We can't come in a fortnight's time," he said. "We are coming tomorrow instead. Is there anything you need? I've just been down to the Customs Office and fetched a big parcel for you. It is full of balls of wool. . . ."

When the nurse got back and told the children the news, none of them were very surprised. "I told you so, didn't I?" said Mfuddla. "And I need some bright red wool, so please may I choose first?"

Scripture

Even before they finish praying to me, I will answer their prayers. Isaiah 65:24

Prayer

"Because you love me, Lord,
And hear me when I pray,
I'll tell you all I need,
And trust you, Lord, today.
Just as a mother loves
To give her children food,
So you delight to give
All that is right and good."—unknown

Reflection

Practice speaking to God in your heart, telling him about your small needs at any time, and always watching to see what he will do.

Chapter 33

THE EMPTY BASKET

*We pray knowing that
God does miracles*

1 Kings 17:8-24

We met Mr. Mattar in the strange and beautiful place where for many years he worked as keeper—the Garden Tomb in Jerusalem. In this place a single old tomb is cut in the face of the rock, and there is a single slab of stone inside where a body was once laid. Outside are the grooves of a great boulder that must once have been rolled across the entrance. There is no stone there now; the grave is open and empty. Because of its structure and position, many people think that this must be the tomb that Joseph of Arimathea gave for the burial of Jesus.

Many tourists come to see the Garden Tomb, and Mr. Mattar, the Arab guardian, used to love to show such visitors round the quiet, beautifully kept garden and talk to them about the gospel story. When we met him, he invited us to a meal, and we asked him how he and his wife had come to be in charge of this place and whether he had been there long. So he told us his story.

Until the time of the partition when Jerusalem was divided into Arab and Jewish sections, Mr. Mattar had been a bank manager. When war broke out, he and his wife and nine children were away from home and, on account of the fighting, were unable to get back. His bank, his house, and all his money were in an area allocated to the Jews, and he and his family were stranded and fast becoming destitute.

"Daily I went to the branch of our bank situated in Jerusalem," he said, "but no money was coming through, and they could not help me. At home we had lived comfortably; my children had never lacked anything. But here in Jerusalem our money was running out fast, and my wife and I were getting worried. Later there was relief organized for the hundreds of refugees, but just then all was in confusion. We did not know where to turn for help.

"But daily we turned to the Lord. We read his promises to ourselves, and we gathered our children and read the promises to them. We read in the Psalms, 'Even lions go hungry for lack of food, but those who obey the Lord lack nothing good.' We read in Isaiah, 'God's people will be free from worries, and their homes peaceful and safe. . . . How happy everyone will be with plenty of water for the crops and safe pasture.' Most of all we trusted the words of Jesus, 'Be concerned above everything else with the Kingdom of God and with what he requires of you, and he will provide you with all these other things.'

"I felt quite sure that God would keep his promises and we would not go hungry. But I wanted my children to be sure of this, too. The day came when we finished the last of our food for breakfast, and once again I spoke to them. 'Children,' I said, 'the Lord has promised to give us what we need, but we have no money and no dinner. So we will tell this to the Lord and to no one else. And I will go out with this empty basket and you will stay at home. Then we shall see whether the promises of God are true or not.'

"So we all prayed round the empty basket. The children understood that this was very important, and they watched me walk down the street with the empty basket in my hand. I did not know where to go, but I decided to look in at the branch of our bank again in case anything was coming through.

"The answer was the same as before. As I turned to go, I found an old friend of mine from my hometown in the queue. He had left the district before the worst troubles and banked his money in Jerusalem.

"'Why, Mattar!' cried my friend. 'What are you doing here?'

"'We now have a small house in Jerusalem,' I replied. 'As we were on holiday when the fighting started, we were not able to get back to our real home outside Jerusalem.'

"'Then you must be having money problems. Tell me, how are you managing?'

"I was about to tell him of our plight when I remembered my words to the children. 'We will tell the Lord and no one else,' I had said. So I told him we were quite all right and left the bank with my empty basket. I did not know where to go next, so I went and sat on a seat in the shade in the park opposite. *I spoke the truth,* I thought to myself. *Those who trust in God are always all right. All will be well.*

"I sat staring at the ground, waiting for a word or a sign. I did not hear when my old friend walked toward me across the grass. 'I don't care what you say, Mattar. You can't be all right with nine kids to feed.' he said. Then he dropped a handful of bank notes into the empty basket and went on his way.

"I rose up and went to the market and filled the basket until it was almost too heavy to carry. I bought all that we needed for a good lunch and much more, and the rest of the money I put in my pocket. Then I went home. It was nearly lunchtime, and the children were waiting at the gate. They stared in wonder at the overflowing basket.

"Then we sat down together and ate our meal. It was good to eat so bountifully after the lean week that had passed, but it was even better to know that the Lord keeps his promises."

Shortly after this Mr. Mattar found work, and, after his children grew up, he and his wife retired to the little bungalow built in the garden of the Resurrection. He became keeper of the tomb and the garden until the Six Days' War when he was shot dead, right by the open door of the grave. Perhaps he, who loved the place so much, would have been glad to die on the very spot where his master conquered death.

And with all his abundant wealth through Christ Jesus, my God will supply all your needs. Philippians 4:19

Prayer

Help me, Father, day by day to believe your promises and to prove that they are true. I pray also for those who are needy and hungry in the world today. Give them today their daily bread. Teach them to turn in faith to you. Show me what I can do to help them.

Reflection

Do you think that you would be happier or better off if God answered yes to all your prayers?

THE BUS THAT WOULD NOT STOP

Wake up, Fatima, we must be starting; the sun is already over the crest of the hill!"

Fatima yawned and sat up. She and Mary had been sleeping in the village where they went every Tuesday evening to give out medicine and to tell the gospel message to any who wanted to hear. Menana, a woman whom Mary had first met in her dispensary, had begged them to come and had gladly welcomed them into her little home. Each Tuesday at sunset the thatched hut filled up with a crowd of dark-eyed villagers on their way home from the fields. Some wanted medicine only, but some would stay on, crouched round the charcoal, asking for Bible stories. Sometimes they would discuss a question far into the night, and it was often after midnight when they lay down to sleep on the mattresses sideling the walls.

Nevertheless, Fatima and Mary had to be up early and get back home as fast as they could, for children arrived there at about nine o'clock for school. Sometimes the two walked the eight-mile distance, but occasionally they caught a rather irregular market bus that would take them about three miles on their way, to a certain fork in the road.

That early summer morning they started off as usual. The harvest had been reaped, and the fields were pale gold stubble. The dawn wind stirred the threshing floors. Down by the river the Indian corn grew in emerald patches, and the figs were ripe for picking. The sky was already bright through the early mists, and they could tell it was going to be very hot. The sooner they got home, the better. To their great relief, the bus, laden with villagers, was in sight as they reached the main road. They managed to squeeze in.

Soon Fatima nudged Mary, for they were getting near the fork in the road. They rose and battled their way to the front.

"Stop, please," called out Fatima. "We want to get off here."

But the driver turned out to be a very surly, unpleasant man. He replied, "I am not going to stop here. This is no proper stopping place. I'm going on to the next bridge. There is another fork there, and you can walk back to your village."

"But that will take us miles out of our way down the valley!" cried Mary. "It will take us hours to walk back up that steep mountainside. Oh, please stop!" And in her heart she cried to God, *Oh, Lord, we need to get home, and it is getting so hot. Please make him stop.*

But the driver would not be persuaded, and there was nothing to do but to go and sit down again. Mary felt very cross indeed, but Fatima was surprisingly calm. "We prayed this morning that all would be well," she said. "We shall get back some time. Let us be patient."

When at last the bus stopped and put them down at the foot of a steep hill seven miles from home, Mary did not feel at all patient. They stood gazing down the valley, hoping another vehicle would appear, but there was nothing in sight. Already the heat was shimmering on the hills, and the river, almost dried up now, trickled between the oleander bushes.

Fatima and Mary never heard the woman approaching. She had walked down the hill behind where they stood, and in her arms was a bundle covered with a cloth. She glanced at Mary, but went straight to Fatima. "Is that the English nurse?" she demanded.

"Yes, my sister," replied Fatima.

"Then present me to her," said the woman.

She was a strong country woman in a shady straw hat, with a striped cloth round her waist. On her legs she wore leather gaiters to protect her from thorns and snakebites, and round her neck she wore charms to protect her from evil spirits. She came straight over to where Mary stood and drew the cloth away from the bundle in her arms. It was a baby whose face she had covered to keep the flies away from its infected eyes. The lids were swollen as large as purple grapes, and they were stuck shut. What the eyes were like underneath had yet to be discovered.

"I have brought her to you," said the woman simply.

"How long has she been like that?" asked Mary.

"Four days. She lies crying with her face to the wall and will not suck."

"But how did you know to come here? It is not market day. There are no others from your village on the road."

"Last night I knew my child was getting worse. She was burning with fever. I slept with a heavy heart, and as I slept, I dreamed. A man came to me dressed all in white, and he said to me, 'Take that child to the English nurse.'

"I said in my dream, 'I do not know where she lives, nor do I know her.'

"And the man in white answered, 'Rise at dawn and go down to the main road by the bridge, and there you will find her waiting for you. She will tell you what to do.'

"So I came and you are here."

The three women set off up the long hill, and soon another bus came and picked them up, making their journey much shorter. The mother stayed with Fatima and Mary all day, and by evening, after penicillin injections and frequent irrigations, her baby looked much better. Then Mary sent medicine home with her and promised to visit on the next Saturday.

The child recovered completely, and the Saturday visit was only the first of many opportunities to speak to that family and village about the love of Jesus. And sitting on the floor that day talking with the mother and her neighbor about the Savior's love, Mary and Fatima thanked God many, many times that he had answered "wait" when Mary had prayed that the bus would stop.

Never doubt that God hears your prayer. If he does not answer at once, trust that he has some good reason. Read the story of Lazarus in John 11. The family wanted Jesus to come at once, but he waited four days in order to do a far greater miracle than healing a sick man. Many believed in him when they saw Lazarus raised from the dead, and Martha and Mary learned important things about Jesus in the waiting time.

Scripture

Jesus answered him, "You do not understand now what I am doing, but you will understand later." John 13:7

Prayer

Lord, I bring to you again those things for which I have prayed and seen no answer. Please strengthen my faith to know that you know and love and care and that you have heard every prayer. Teach me to be patient and to wait for your time, because you know best what is right for me.

Thank you that one day I shall understand why you said wait or no. But help me to trust you in the meantime, Father.

Reflection

Can you think of an instance when a delayed answer to your prayer has finally brought about better results?

THE LOST LEADER

Everyone knew Stephen. He was one of the Christians, and he had been made director of the Christians' social services program, giving out food supplies to the widows. The process had not been too well organized before, and there had been a few problems with the old ladies: the Greek immigrants had accused the Christians of racism and of favoring the Hebrews. But since Stephen had been put in charge of a small food-distribution group, there had been no more complaints. The widows were delighted and looked upon young Stephen as their provider.

But food distribution was only a part-time job. Stephen's heart was burning with love for Jesus of Nazareth, the unrecognized Messiah of the Jews, who had recently been crucified outside the city walls. Because this man named Jesus was also God, not even a stone-sealed grave had been able to hold him. He had risen from the dead and gone back to his Father in heaven. But, before he went, he had entrusted his disciples with this message: "Go throughout the whole world and preach the gospel to all mankind."

Stephen, brokenhearted because he had been so slow to recognize who Jesus was, now took every opportunity to preach the Good News. No one could stop him. The moment the last widow had left and the place had been tidied up, Stephen was off!

Those were wonderful days; it was as though Christ lived again in his followers. His love and power shone out through Stephen. When he spoke, it was almost as though Jesus were speaking through him. But the proud rulers who had hated Jesus, hated him again in this young Christian and tried to silence Stephen by threats and arguments. When this failed, they bribed false witnesses to tell lies about him. On their false evidence, the rulers were finally able to arrest Stephen and take him into custody.

Hundreds attended Stephen's trial and heard the lies that were told about him. Watching him as he listened to their accusations, his enemies must have trembled with awe, for God's glory shone out through Stephen. His face was radiant and shining. "It is like an angel's face!" whispered one of the frightened people.

"Are these accusations true?" asked the high priest, who was at least giving

Stephen a chance to defend himself. If he was very tactful, very careful, he might yet escape. It was his last chance.

But looking round on the sea of angry, frightened faces, Stephen thought, *This is my last chance to tell them about my living Lord Jesus. This is no time to be careful.* So, casting caution to the winds, he made the long impassioned speech recorded in the seventh chapter of Acts in the New Testament. He explained how one could trace Israel's refusal to listen to God's voice all through their national history, and he described God's grace and mercy illustrated in always giving them a second chance. He pointed out to the assembly how God's great last offer to mankind, his own Son, had been spurned and crucified. Of course, God had extended his grace yet again—by means of his Holy Spirit—but Stephen never reached that point in his discourse. The mutterings had been getting louder and louder, and suddenly, grinding their teeth and shaking their fists in fury, the Jewish leaders surged forward.

Surely there were Christians in the crowd praying, "Lord, save him; protect him; keep him from harm or death."

Could there be a more terrifying situation? One man alone facing a howling mob out for his blood! Yet Stephen did not even appear to see all that. He was gazing steadfastly upwards at the glory of God. The gate of heaven was open, and Stephen looked right in. "Look, look!" he cried. "I can see heaven open, and Jesus, like a man, standing at God's right hand."

Perhaps the bystanders were gazing up too, but they only saw blue sky. And the rulers had had enough. Blocking their ears to drown that cry of triumph, they grabbed hold of Stephen. Pushed, kicked, punched, now on his feet, now on the ground, he was dragged outside the city. There the angry group, after flinging their coats at the feet of a man called Saul, began to hurl stones at Stephen.

And the Christians no doubt cried, "Oh, Lord, save him from death! We need him! Keep him safe, we pray."

Stephen fell on his knees. The stones were coming thick and fast now, but the gate of heaven was still open. His Master was standing to welcome him, and he was almost home. "Receive my spirit, Lord," he cried, as a spent runner reaching the winner tape cries out for joy and victory. He was almost there, received into love, while behind him there was atrocious evil and hatred. The love and forgiveness of Christ in him flowed back to them. "Don't charge them for this, Lord," he whispered, and falling to the ground, he died.

The angry crowds dispersed. It was probably evening before the frightened, weeping Christians dared to creep out and bury him. They had prayed for his safety, but he had died. God had not heard or answered . . . or had he? Could it be that, yes, their prayers had been heard all the time, that heaven's gate had been flung open in answer and Stephen had been gloriously saved and protected—saved from fear, saved from defeat, saved, above all, from hate? Had not love conquered right to the last so that Stephen, saved from death, now reigned in eternal life?

Back in his home, that proud Jew named Saul struggled with his fear and conscience and fought against God. He had been watching while guarding the clothes of those who were stoning Stephen. Saul hated this Jesus. But tonight he had been badly shaken. . . . What had Stephen seen? How could a man die like that in peace and love?

The Christians had lost a leader through Stephen's death, but God was preparing another one. For though he did not know it, Saul was soon to yield to Christ.

There can be several reasons why God sometimes says no to our prayers. But the reason is never that he did not hear or that the request was not important enough. Usually God's no means that a yes would not have been good and right for us. But sometimes he says no because he has a far better answer than the one asked for, as in this story. Many were helped by Stephen's life, but millions have been helped by Stephen's death. Although we cannot always see how things will work out at the time, we need to trust that one day we shall understand and we shall praise God for having answered our prayer in his own way—the very best way.

Scripture

I depend on God alone; I put my hope in him. He alone protects and saves me; he is my defender. Psalm 62:5-6

Prayer

Father, I want to tell you that I will trust you about the prayers that have not been answered. I trust that you hear and love me and know best. I trust that you are quietly working out a better answer than the one I wanted, and I thank you that one day I shall understand.

Reflection

Have you ever felt let down when God answered no to your prayer? Can you look back yet and see that God was planning a better answer than the one you wanted?

Chapter 36

SONG AT MIDNIGHT

*We pray giving thanks
and praise to God*

Acts 16

They leaned back against the rough stone wall keeping very still; the least movement was painful, and their feet were firmly held in stocks, making movement almost impossible anyway. It was pitch-dark there in the heart of prison, but the long, agonizing night was still ahead of them. What the morning might bring they did not know, but it might well be execution. Still, they looked backwards rather than forwards, for their minds were full of the amazing, glorious, and terrible events of the past few weeks.

They talked softly about all that had happened, glad that they were fettered close together. They remembered the day they had arrived in Philippi, two weary travelers uncertain of what to do next, but very sure that God had led them. Then came that quiet Sabbath morning when they had walked to the valley between the hills where the river flowed and found that little group of women praying, Lydia among them.

Lydia! They had hardly to explain anything, for Lydia's heart was already wide open to the truth about Jesus. She had been the first to believe, and her home quickly became a center for preaching and hearing the gospel. Then others believed, and little groups of Christians began gathering there, eager for teaching. It all seemed so bright . . . until the incident of the slave girl, and that too seemed such a wonderful victory for Jesus. The unclean spirit had been driven out of her, and she became so gentle, so changed. But her masters were furious. No one would be paying to hear the evil spirit speak any longer. The girl had become a dead loss to them, and of course they blamed those pestilential new teachers for the whole thing.

So Paul and Silas had suddenly been attacked in the street and dragged to the courthouse in the marketplace, where they were accused of disturbing the peace. Nobody would listen to what they tried to say. They were simply beaten with rods there and then and thrown into the town jail.

"Make absolutely sure they don't escape," the magistrates ordered the jailer. "Strange things have been happening, and you can't be too careful. . . ."

"Oh, I'll be careful all right," the jailer assured them. "Nothing strange is going to happen in my prison; I'll even put their feet in the stocks for good measure."

So there they were, stiff, sore, and bewildered. It had all taken place so quickly. They did not really mind what happened to them, for they were used to that sort of thing. But what about Lydia and the new Christians, and what about the newly exorcised slave girl?

"We'll pray for them," said Paul, for he knew that neither stocks nor bars nor stone ceilings could prevent prayer from rising up to God. And as they prayed, they forgot the pain and darkness, and Christ himself seemed to draw near and stand beside them in the cell—the Christ who had suffered far more even than they, whose voice had guided them to Philippi, whose power had saved Lydia and cast out the demon, whose healing, comforting love was round about them in the prison.

Suddenly it all seemed so wonderful that Silas and Paul broke into singing. They just could not help it! Louder and louder rose those happy songs of praise, and the prisoners woke from sleep and sat up to listen, for no one had ever heard singing in that prison before. More important, God was listening too, for there is great power in praise, and Satan cannot stand before it. As the music echoed through the prison, the foundations began to shake, bolts and locks were strained, and iron doors flew open with a crash. Chains snapped and fell with a clatter to the ground, and the frightened prisoners groped for the passages. They were suddenly free, but it was too dark to see which way to go.

No one was more frightened than the jailer, for he knew that if one prisoner escaped, he would pay with his life. Roman execution was cruel and gruesome. It would be far better to die there in the prison, alone in the night. He drew his sword to pierce his own heart, and all his dark, evil life rose up before him. . . . Where was he going? Could anything save him from the punishment of the gods?

Then a voice came clear through the darkness, "Don't kill yourself! No one has escaped. We are all here."

The jailer's fear increased. He knew that voice. It was the voice of one of the prisoners who had sung in the dark and who had not feared death. Wait. Perhaps those two had found the answer to death, and perhaps they would tell him their secret. "Bring lights!" he screamed, and, while the other prison officials ran in with lanterns and secured the cells, he rushed to the place where the voice had spoken. Paul and Silas stood in the glow, masters of the situation, and the trembling jailer fell at their feet. "Sirs!" he cried. "What must I do to be saved?"

Strong and certain the answer rang out: "Believe in the Lord Jesus Christ and you will be saved—you and your family."

So that was the secret! There in the prison, the jailer washed their wounds and woke his sleeping family, for the time was short. Paul and Silas, who must have been longing to lie down and rest, told them about Jesus and baptized them as Christians. Then the jailer took them to his home, and they all had a meal together and rejoiced. It was a strange, wonderful night, and the dawn came all too soon. Already the rumors were all over the town, and the frightened magistrates were apologizing and beseeching Paul and Silas to leave the town at once.

Something very strange had indeed happened in the prison! And all because two prisoners had looked up to God in the pain and darkness and given him thanks and praise.

———●✦✦●———

Three simple words can serve to help you remember three kinds of prayer— these are *sorry, please,* and *thank you. Sorry* can stand for prayers of repentance. As we remember anything that has displeased or grieved God, we can ask him to forgive us. *Please* can stand for prayers of intercession, when we ask God for help and bring our own needs or the needs of others to him. *Thank you* can stand for prayers of praise and gratitude, when we remember who God is and all that he has done for us, for those we love, and for the world.

Scripture

[David's prayer of thanksgiving:] Praise the Lord, my soul! All my being, praise his holy name! Praise the Lord, my soul, and do not forget how kind he is. He forgives all my sins and heals all my diseases. He keeps me from the grave and blesses me with love and mercy. He fills my life with good things, so that I stay young and strong like an eagle. Psalm 103:1-5

Reflection

Try to write a prayer of thanksgiving in your own words, that you could keep and use again and again. Thank God for things you are particularly grateful for, and perhaps also things you dislike but know he is using for your good.

Chapter 37

When we serve others,
we are serving God

Matthew 25:31-46

THE CHRISTMAS GUEST

This story is a legend from the ancient Orthodox Church and tells about a cobbler named Gregory.

Gregory lived in a village where for many years he had mended the shoes of the whole community. Six days a week he worked hard, but on Sunday he always shut up shop and climbed to the little church on the hilltop to pray and praise God. Sundays were his happiest days, for the Lord was his very best friend.

The years went by, and Gregory became an old man. His wife had died, and his children had married and gone away. He could no longer work as long or as swiftly as before. Money was becoming scarce; sometimes he barely had enough to buy food and firewood.

One year at Christmas time, when thick snow lay on the roofs and blanketed the hills, the village people were hurrying up to the church to celebrate Christ's birth and rejoice together. The lamps were all lighted, and their orange glow streamed from the church windows. Only old Gregory, the cobbler, sat at the window of his shop, watching the happy throng with a wistful expression on his face. Many stopped to greet him. "Are you not coming, Father Gregory? The bells are ringing; get your cloak and come with us."

But Gregory shook his head sadly. "I can no longer come climb the hill," he said. "My knees are so stiff with rheumatism that I can barely cross the street."

He sat for a long time listening to the bells and the far music of Christmas hymns coming to him over the frosty air. He felt weak and old and soon fell into a deep sleep. As he slept, he dreamed that an angel stood by his bed, and the whole room glowed with the warmth and light of his presence. "What is your wish, Gregory?" asked the angel. "Just say it, for your desire will be granted."

Gregory answered boldly, "I cannot go with the people to the house of God, so I ask that the Christ child himself will visit me in my home."

"Tomorrow your wish shall be granted," said the angel, and the light faded.

Gregory woke in the cold, gray dawn. The snow lay fresh and beautiful in the streets, but Gregory had no time to look outside. He knew that his dream had spoken truth, that today he would welcome his heavenly guest. There was no time to lose, for he had much to do. Painfully he swept the room, laid the firewood, and put out what food he had on a snowy cloth. He would neither eat nor light the fire until his guest arrived. When all was ready, he went and sat in his little shop window, shading his eyes and scanning the street from left to right.

Someone was coming. His heart missed a beat and then steadied. It was no Christ child, only the small son of the blind man who lived down the road. He was limping barefoot in the snow, and as he came nearer, Gregory saw that his knuckles were pressed to his eyes. The child was crying softly. The cobbler leant from his window.

"Why are you crying, child?"

"Because of the chilblains on my feet; they hurt me so!"

"But why do you walk barefoot in the snow?"

"Because we have no firewood and I am going to buy a little."

"But where are your shoes?"

"I have grown out of them. They pinch my chilblains."

"Then come here, child; come into the shop; lay your foot on this leather. Today I am expecting a guest, but tomorrow I will make you a pair of sandals. Come back in two days' time. . . . No, you need not bring any money. Your father is my friend."

The child's eyes shone through his tears, and he ran off, his pain forgotten. The pale winter sun was now high overhead, and still the guest had not arrived. Anxiously Gregory scanned the street. Yes, someone was coming! He gazed intently, and then gave a sigh of disappointment. It was only the widow from the back alley, taking her bread home. She had been out early, begging, and she bade him good day. He suddenly remembered that he had mended some shoes for her.

"Widow Mary," he called. "Why do you not collect your shoes? They have been ready this long time past."

"I cannot pay for them, Father Gregory," she replied. "I have six little mouths to feed. You had better sell them and take your fee. These must last me till the snow melts."

He looked at the tattered sandals on her feet. "Take these, Widow Mary," he said, holding out her shoes. "The little ones need the money more than I do. Take them in Christ's name, and God bless you!"

Her tired face brightened. Tears of gratitude rolled down her thin cheeks. She kissed his hand and went on her way, blessing him. The sun sank toward the yellowing west, and still the Christ child did not come.

Sunset came, cold and beautiful, with the little church silhouetted black against an orange sky, gray shadows on the snow. He would not come now. . . . Perhaps it was all just a dream. . . . Cold and hungry, the old man took a last look down the road.

Someone was coming, but it was no radiant child. It was a tired traveler, leaning on his staff and looking about him. He was a stranger, and Gregory called to him. "Where are you going, traveler?"

"To my son's house in the next village. But I have another five miles to walk, and I am faint with cold and hunger. May I rest a little in the shelter of your home?"

"Come in and welcome," said Gregory, opening the door. The traveler sank down beside the unlighted fire. He was shivering, and his fingers were blue. Gregory hesitated. "I would gladly light the fire, brother," he said, "but I am expecting a guest."

"A guest? Who would come so late at night through the snow? I would fain warm my hands."

Gregory went to the window for the last time. *He will not come now*, he thought sadly. *I was deceived by a dream. How can I now refuse food and warmth to this poor stranger?* He lit the fire, and the traveler revived in the cheerful glow.

"I will finish my journey in the morning," said the traveler. "Blessing on you, my friend, for your kindness to the poor stranger."

Gregory lay down to sleep, but his heart was heavy with disappointment. Had the angel deceived him? Sorrowfully he whispered into the darkness, "Why did you not come, Lord? All day I waited. . . ."

And once again the darkness seemed invaded by warmth and brightness, and a voice spoke out, "But I did come! And what a royal welcome you gave me!" And then it seemed as though voices were singing all about him, and the words he heard were these:

> "For I was the child with the bleeding feet,
> And I was the widow who wept in the street,
> And I was the stranger who asked for meat."

In the Gospel of Matthew (25:31-45) you will see that the best way to serve and love Jesus is to serve and love other people. All that we do for his sake is treasured and remembered in heaven. But all that we fail to do for others, grieves God.

Scripture

I tell you, whenever you did this for one of the least important of these brothers of mine, you did it for me! Matthew 25:40

Prayer

Lord, you come to me in many different people every day.
Teach me to love and give and serve each of them for your sake.

How would it change your behavior today if you remembered that whatever you say or do to a person, you are actually saying or doing to Jesus?

Chapter 38 # LI'S ROPE

*We lead others to the
light of Christ*

2 Corinthians 5:14-21

He came limping along the street, his stick tapping, his begging bowl lifted, and his nearly blind eyes peering at the light. He was incredibly ragged, dirty, and footsore, and he seemed lost. Where the road divided he stood still.

"Will someone lead me to the Place of Heavenly Healing?" he called in his beggar's whine, and a child plucked at his sleeve and led him to the hospital gate. Tapping on the gate with his stick, he asked admittance.

"But the beds are all full," said the gatekeeper.

"Then I will lie in the courtyard till one is empty," said poor Li. "Only you must feed me, for I have come many, many miles seeing only the light ahead and the dust at my feet, begging and begging all the way. Many days I have been on the road, but all told me that I should find mercy here."

The gatekeeper shuffled off and fetched the doctor, who came and looked at Li. It was quite true, the beds were full, but the beggar's story also sounded true. His bruised and calloused feet and his exhaustion were the evidence. "Get him washed, and put a mattress in the passageway," said the doctor.

So Li was admitted. For the first time in many years he slept on a mattress and ate good food three times a day. It was like heaven. Then, a few days later, he went trustfully to the operating room where the cataracts were removed from his eyes. And, when the bandages were taken off, he was given a pair of spectacles. Li could see!

But there was more to the story than that. A lonely outcast, Li had known nothing of love since his childhood. It was partly his longing for sight and partly the lure of the name, *The Place of Heavenly Healing*, that had made him take that long, weary, dangerous journey. Now, evening by evening, after they had eaten their rice, the hospital patients gathered round to sing and listen, and the story they were told of the love of God revealed in Jesus seemed to be the answer to all of Li's unconscious seeking. He felt as though his whole self, body, soul, and spirit had found the light of a new day. Truly, he had been healed.

Li stayed for a long time. He could see, and he should have gone, but, while he gave up his bed to a sick man, he lingered on, camping in an outbuilding and doing small jobs. There was so much to learn, and those who taught him rejoiced at his understanding. Perhaps, later, he could train to be an evangelist.

Then, abruptly, Li announced that he was going home. When questioned, he was rather vague about his plans. Asked if he was going back to teach in his own village, he replied that he did not think he knew enough to tell others. He only knew that he must go, but one day he would come back. Bowing with the greatest respect, he left early one morning, and those at the hospital watched him go rather sadly, for they did not think he would return.

It was many weeks later when Li came back. The village and hospital were quiet; it was the hot season and the time of the afternoon siesta. Suddenly, people woke, startled, and ran to their doors, hearing the sound of tapping of sticks. The gatekeeper glanced up, rubbed his eyes, and then gave a gasp of horror and ran for the doctor. "Come!" he cried. "Come and see! They are all heading for the hospital. What will you do with them all?"

The doctor ran to the door, his wife behind him. What they saw was Li, walking confidently down the road, spectacles on nose. In his hand he held a rope, tied to the wrist of a blind beggar who shuffled along behind holding a begging bowl and stick. The rope on his wrist was attached to the wrist of another blind beggar, who in turn led another. . . . In all, there were some fifteen of them. Li had started off with three or four of his old comrades, and they had picked up another beggar in almost every village they had passed through. Managing to survive on scraps of food given to them along the way, the stumbling little procession had finally arrived at the hospital.

"How could I not tell them?" exclaimed Li proudly. "I who have seen the light!"

They all rested and were fed in the shade of the tree in the hospital yard, and then all were examined. Some were admitted and regained their sight, and some were given treatment to relieve their pain. Sad to say, not all of them could be healed physically, but all heard of the love of Jesus. It was a busy, difficult time for the doctor and the already overworked hospital staff, but they were not sorry at all. For Li had come back. He had surely understood what the Lord Jesus meant when he said to his disciples, "Go throughout the whole world and preach the gospel to all mankind."

———————●·•··•·●———————

If we believe, we need to ask ourselves in the same way as Li, how can we keep silent? How can we not tell them—all our friends who have not yet seen and received the light of the gospel? Jesus said that we are the light of the world, showing him to others as a lantern radiates the light that is shining inside it. We who have seen the light must show others Jesus.

Scripture

Help me to speak, Lord, and I will praise you. Psalm 51:15

Father, I pray for my friends, especially those who are not interested in Jesus and who know nothing about the love of God. Show me how I can lead them to your light. Make me faithful in praying for them. Help me to live out Christ's love, and, when the opportunity comes, help me to tell them about the difference you have made to me.

Reflection

Think of a friend of yours who knows nothing about Jesus. What can you do or say to show him or her the light of Christ?

Chapter 39

We can all take part in spreading the Good News to the whole world

Romans 10:6-18

THE GIRL WHO DID NOT FORGET

Nicola had had a wonderful summer holiday, the best ever! Night after night, back in England later, she would lie in bed and relive the joyful crowded hours.

In a way it had not been a holiday at all; it had been a working party—they had traveled in a jeep and a Volkswagen van through France and Spain, crossed the Straits of Gibraltar in a boat, and landed in North Africa. There they had camped in two empty wards of a mission hospital (the patients had been sent home for a month), which they had redecorated. The trip had been organized by their Bible study leader, and they had joined two other groups, so Nicola had made a lot of new friends.

Of course, it had not been all work. At midday, when the heat was almost overpowering, they would put down their tools, grab a picnic lunch, bundle into the cars, and make for the beaches—those vast Mediterranean beaches where the sand was too hot to walk on barefoot, and where the water was so calm they could see every pebble on the sandy bottom. Or sometimes they would drive farther to where the great Atlantic breakers thundered on the shore and the surf picked them up like rag dolls and flung them back on the beach.

At five o'clock they would start another spell of work—Nicola loved painting hospital lockers—and then they would take their supper into the garden where they ate looking across at those amazing sunsets over the sea. Afterwards they would gather round to talk or to study their Bibles. Sometimes one of the hospital staff would come up and tell them about the work of the mission hospital, and some of these talks were unforgettable to Nicola. What must it be like, she wondered, to become a Christian and then to have your Bible torn up, or to be turned out of school or sent to prison because of your faith? And there were other problems too. What must it be like to see your baby hungry and not be able to buy milk for it? Nicola wanted to help, but what could she do?

It was nine months after the trip, at the beginning of the summer term, that Nicola had her bright idea. It all started with her memory of one of the hospital

126

workers telling about a mission summer camp there in North Africa. Different age groups came to the camp for a week each. In the morning they had Bible lessons, and in the afternoon they went to the beach. Few of the children boasted a bathing costume, so they often had to swim in turns to make what was available go round.

While Nicola was remembering all this, the lack of swimming attire had actually gotten to be quite serious in the mission camp. The children listened in dismay as the worker in charge told them, "You must all bring something of your own to swim in. The old bathing costumes are worn out. I let you keep some last year, and there are hardly any left. If you can't produce something, you just won't be able to swim. You little ones, can't you swim in your pants?"

The little girls looked profoundly shocked and assured her that at seven years old, such a thing was not to be thought of.

There seemed no solution. Swimsuits were impossibly expensive, almost the price of a weekly family food allowance for some. They went home despondent, and those in charge prayed about the need. It was then, without any warning, that Nicola's parcel arrived with a letter enclosed:

> I don't suppose you'll remember, but I was in the summer working party last year, and you spoke to us one night. I just could not forget those children swimming in turns. At the beginning of this term a lot of my friends turned out in new swimsuits, and I asked them what they'd done with their old swimsuits. When I explained why I wanted them, half of the class produced old bathing things of some sort, so we send them with our love.

The letter was simply signed "Nicky."

I was there when that parcel arrived. And, Nicky, I wish you could have seen the riot that broke out when the children saw the contents of your package! It took some time to restore order. I wish you could have watched them skimming over the sands in their bright costumes or seen them listening quietly to the stories or singing the choruses! I wish you could have seen the wonder in their eyes when we told them how we had prayed for a parcel! You would have thought all the trouble of putting together that parcel and the heavy cost of the postage so worthwhile. Thank you, Nicky!

Scripture

There are other sheep which belong to me that are not in this sheep pen. I must bring them, too; they will listen to my voice, and they will become one flock with one shepherd. John 10:16

Prayer

"I know in distant countries
Across the deep blue sea,
Are many other children
You love as you love me.
But they have never heard your Name
And do not know that Jesus came.

Lord, help me send the message
Across the deep blue sea,
To tell those other children
What you have done for me.
Oh, show me Lord, what I can do
That they may know and love you too."—unknown

Reflection

You do not always know what seeds you are sowing, nor do you always see the result of your efforts. But, remember this—so much can be reaped from even the smallest kind deed.

Chapter 40

Chapter 40

*We give to God freely
out of love and gratitude
to him*

Malachi 3:10

THE LORD'S WHITE CHICKEN

This is a story from Syria, where many years ago a young American couple set up their home in a country district and began to preach the gospel.

The people in the villages round were mostly farmers and shepherds, and they worshiped God. But they had never read a Bible, and they did not know that their sins could be forgiven by trusting in Christ. These things were wonderful to them, and night after night they would gather from the fields, tired, hot, and earthy, to sit and listen while Ralph taught them from the Bible. Many believed what they heard and asked the Holy Spirit to come into their lives. One night as they talked about the love of God in giving Jesus and the love of Jesus in giving his life, one of the Syrian Christians asked, "But what can we give to show that we, too, love him?"

"We hardly have any money," some observed, "and what we have we must spend on our farming tools and our work. We all know we are poor and must live on our farm produce. Sometimes, in winter, we can scarcely even find bread for our children, so how and what can we give?"

Ralph turned to the book of Malachi and spoke of a time long ago when God told his people to bring a tenth of all that they had for the work of God. But the people got lazy and greedy and began keeping everything for themselves. So the prophet Malachi gave them a message from God: "Bring the full amount of your tithes to the Temple, so that there will be plenty of food there. Put me to the test and you will see that I will open the windows of heaven and pour out on you in abundance all kinds of good things" (Malachi 3:10).

The village people looked at each other. "A tenth of our corn, our eggs, our fruit?" they asked doubtfully. "But what if we haven't enough for ourselves?"

"What does the passage say?" asked Ralph.

"It says that the Lord will open the windows of heaven and pour us out an abundance of good things. . . . It sounds good. . . . But is it true?"

"Try it and see," said Ralph.

So they tried. Each brought a tenth of his produce to Ralph, who bought it and either lived on it or sold it and set the price of it aside. Soon there was enough money to buy building materials, and they built themselves a little church where they met to worship. Joy and blessing came to the village, and it was easy to give. They longed to go to other villages to tell of their newfound Savior, but they could not leave their flocks and fields. If they saved up more money, perhaps they could pay for one of their number to go. The little store of gifts began to grow again.

Then there came a time of drought; gifts became fewer. Somehow the spirit of the little congregation seemed less joyful, and the leaders of the church were troubled.

Someone else was troubled too. At a small farm nearby lived a widow whose husband had died of typhoid fever, leaving her with three little children. Her life was hard, but she had a patch of land, a goat, and about thirty hens. With these she eked out a living. But during the past year she had learned about Christ in her simple way, and life had been different since she had learned to take her needs to him in prayer.

It was a great day when she found her white hen sitting on a clutch of eggs. Instinctively she would have put one aside for the Lord, but, *Better give the Lord a chicken than an egg,* she thought. Sure enough, a little while later, ten beautiful yellow chickens hatched out. She caught one at once and tied a piece of sheep's wool round its leg.

"Why are you doing that?" asked her nine-year-old daughter, Mariam.

"Because it is the Lord's chicken," replied her mother, "and we must look after it carefully."

The chicks grew, and Mariam loved them dearly. "When are you going to give the Lord his chicken, my mother?" she asked.

"Not yet, my daughter. Let it grow; better give the Lord a hen than a chick."

Then a very surprising thing happened. All the chickens grew fine and strong, but the Lord's chicken grew finer and stronger than all the rest. It was truly a prize chicken, its flesh so firm and its feathers so white. Mariam was glad, for to her it seemed right, but her mother was not glad at all. In this year of drought, the crops were so poor, the wheat so stunted, and the tomatoes so shriveled, the Lord's chicken would have fetched an excellent price in the market.

"I was a fool to tie that sheep's wool round the hen's leg," she said to herself several times a day. "After all, Mr. Ralph only said a chicken. He never said which chicken. I could have given the Lord that scraggy dark one. No one would ever have known."

And the matter weighed upon her so heavily that early one Sunday morning she went out to the run and took the wool off the leg of the Lord's chicken and tied it on the leg of the scraggy one. Then she threw her veil over her head, spruced up her three children, and set off to the new little church building for the morning services.

They did not always have a Communion service at the end of their morning worship, but that Sunday they did. A Syrian Christian walked up to the plain wooden table where the bread and wine lay in memory of the body and blood of the Lord Jesus Christ. Before calling the people to come and partake, he gave out a hymn that had been translated into Arabic:

"I gave my life for you,
My precious blood I shed,
That you might ransomed be
And quickened from the dead.
I gave my life for you,
What have you given for me?"

Sweetly and sadly the question at the end of each verse hung on the air. Before the hymn was over there was a disturbance in the church. The widow came to the front, her face buried in her hands, weeping bitterly, talking incoherently. But try as they might, no one could quite understand what she was trying to say. Only three repeated words were really intelligible—"The Lord's chicken! The Lord's chicken!" And in the end, it was Mariam who explained what was the matter with her mother.

Running forward, shyness forgotten, she put her arm round her mother's waist. "She says, 'Wait!'" whispered Mariam. "Wait till she has been home. She wants to put the wool back on the leg of God's chicken. She doesn't want to take the bread and wine till she has done this."

Nobody smiled. People were beginning to understand. The widow lifted her tear-stained face. "He gave so much," she whispered. "I only wanted to give him my worst. How can I remember him? Wait, oh wait . . . I want to give my best."

Others rose quietly to their feet. God's Spirit was working.

"Brother Ralph," said one. "I too want to go home. I have not paid my tenth of wheat. How can I remember his giving?"

"Nor I," murmured another. "I feared the drought. I have not given milk to the Lord for many weeks."

Another called out, "Brothers and sisters, let us not take the Communion this morning. Perhaps many of us need to go home. Let us meet again this evening." Everyone agreed, and they separated in silence.

Ralph got no rest that afternoon, for the people were queuing at the door with their gifts, and in the evening the church was overflowing. Joy and praise had come back to the village. Christ seemed so near, and they were so happy. Mariam and her mother were there, and the widow's eyes were bright with tears as she remembered the love that gave all. Together they sang the hymn:

"Lord, let my life be given,
And every moment spent
For God, for souls, for heaven,

And all earth ties be rent.
You gave your all for me,
Now I give all to you."

And down in the little farm, the Lord's white chicken strutted proudly to and fro with a new piece of sheep's wool tied round its leg.

Scripture

Remembering the words that the Lord Jesus himself said, "There is more happiness in giving than in receiving." Acts 20:35

Prayer

"We thank you then our Father,
For all things bright and good,
The seed-time and the harvest,
Our life, our health, our food.
Accept the gifts we offer,
For all your love imparts,
And, what you most desire,
Our loving, thankful hearts."
—Matthias Claudius

Reflection

God never fails to bless those who give, whether it is their time, their money, their effort, or even sometimes their very life. But God's rewards do not necessarily take the form we expect. If you want to give to God, you must be prepared to do so freely and willingly, out of love. You must give without expecting anything in return, while fully trusting that God will bless you in his own time and in his own way.

THE BOY WHO FEARED THE LIGHT

It was nearly Christmas time, and the weather was dark and stormy. Dave and Billy, hurrying home on the last day of term, longed to linger in front of the bright shop windows, but the streetlamps were already lit and the lane leading up to the farm where they lived was full of ruts and puddles, so they knew they had better get home before it was completely dark.

"Come on, Bill," urged Dave impatiently, but little Bill felt he was in fairyland. He could not pull himself away from the window of a toy shop . . . if only he could have that little garage under the tree . . . and a few of those mini models in his stocking. He had quite forgotten Dave, who waited at the corner where they turned off from the main street into the lane.

Suddenly Dave noticed something that made him forget Billy. He was standing beside an enormous barrow of oranges, lovely and golden in the light of the streetlamp. The owner of the barrow had his back to him, putting up a sign about Jaffa oranges, and there was no one else there at all. It was getting near closing time, and everyone was hurrying home to their teas, but the orange man stayed on for the commuters on the later train.

Dave was all alone with hundreds of beautiful, shining Christmas oranges.

He put out his hand cautiously and tumbled three or four of them into his school bag. Nothing happened. He stuffed four into his pockets. No one had seen. He grabbed five more and stuffed them into his anorak. All was quiet; the stall keeper had not turned round. Dave just could not believe his good luck.

He realized, however, that he was looking extremely fat, and the quicker he could get into the dark lane, the better off he would be. Billy was approaching slowly, his eyes misty, seeing nothing but mini cars, but even so . . . Dave made a run for the high hedges and deep shadows. No one would notice his shape here. He would slip into the barn before entering the house and hide his treasure. Then he could go back whenever he liked, snuggle down in the soft, dusty hay, and eat oranges. It was going to be a wonderful Christmas.

Then Billy, who was afraid of the dark, gave a little cry of joy. "Look! The lantern!" he shouted. "Dad's come to meet us!" Bill ran forward. Dave froze.

"You there?" called their father. "Dark's come early tonight, and you'll be falling into the puddles. Come and walk by me, Dave."

Dave shrank against the hedge, frightened and miserable. He had never thought of this horror. He could not face his upright, honest Dad while hugging his guilty secret. Soon Billy was skipping along in the lantern light, holding his father's hand, all fear forgotten. But Dave slunk along behind.

"What's the matter, Dave?" called his father, who knew his sons very well. "You've been a bad boy today?"

"Dave's been good today," said Billy loyally. "Teacher said he was the best runner in the class. Dad, you know my stocking . . ."

"Dave, come here and walk in the light. You'll stumble there in the ditch."

"I'm okay, Dad."

"Now don't be daft, Davie! You'll get your shoes in a terrible muck. . . ."

"I like walking here. . . . Oh! . . . Ow!" Dave had caught his foot in a root and gone down flat on his nose. The oranges rolled out of his bag in all directions, and the ones in his anorak squashed with a horrible squelch. His father stepped back to the side of the lane and lifted the lantern. Dave burst into wild, frightened sobs.

"I see!" said his father grimly. He picked Dave up and stood him in the light. His hands and knees were badly grazed, his mouth was full of gravel, and his lip was bleeding. He looked so wretched and scared that his father wondered if perhaps he had already been punished enough.

"You took 'em from Sam Smith's stall, didn't you?" the boys' father asked.

"Y-y-yes," sobbed Dave.

"You stole them, Davie, and you're going back right now to pay for them."

"B-but . . . I haven't any money . . . and . . . and . . . he might call the police!"

"That's up to him. If Sam Smith calls the police, it's no more than you deserve. For the moment, here's some money. You go right back and tell Sam what you did and ask him how much a dozen oranges cost. Bill and I will wait for you at the corner."

Sam was very surprised when a terrified, mud-covered young boy suddenly appeared out of the dark and sobbed out his story. He took the money and told Dave that if ever he caught him at such tricks again, he'd call the police at once. When Dave had turned away, Sam winked broadly at the boys' father, who was standing under the next streetlamp.

Suddenly, it was all over. Of course Dave would have to pay the money back from his own pocket money, but somehow that did not seem to matter much. The oranges were paid for, and he was forgiven. He was limping up the lane by the light of the lantern, sniffing and hiccupping and very sore, but his father's arm was round him, helping him over the puddles.

"Never do a thing like that again, Davie," said his father. "It just doesn't pay. See?"

And Dave, clinging to his dad, vowed that he never, never would.

———◆◆◆◆◆———

If we sin, we cannot walk in the light with Jesus. When you know there is something on your conscience, you need to confess it and put it right with God quickly. Then you will be cleared and forgiven, and you will come back to walk with Jesus.

Scripture

[Jesus said,] "I have come into the world as light, so that everyone who believes in me should not remain in the darkness." John 12:46

The light has come into the world, but people love the darkness rather than the light, because their deeds are evil. John 3:19

If we live in the light—just as he is in the light—then we have fellowship with one another, and the blood of Jesus, his Son, purifies us from every sin. 1 John 1:7

Prayer

O Lord, I pray that I may never allow unconfessed sin to come between me and you. Keep me walking in the light with Jesus with nothing to hide. Keep me close to Jesus.

Reflection

No sin that you ever do is too small or too great for God's forgiving love.

Chapter 42

OUT OF THE FIRE

*We need other Christians
and they need us*

1 Corinthians 12

Jonathan had become a Christian at camp, but he did not feel he was getting on very well. At first he had felt so happy and had enjoyed learning from his Bible and his Bible studyguide and had found it easy to pray. It was all new and exciting. He was more helpful at home, easier to get on with, kinder, and more careful about what he said.

This did not last, unfortunately. The mornings were getting colder, and it was harder to get up; he was finding his daily Bible reading and prayer rather a bore. He had made friends with a boy at school who laughed at religion, and Jonathan felt lonely and disappointed. Perhaps he had just imagined all that had happened at camp; perhaps there had been nothing real about it.

Before he completely gave up on the new life he had heard about at camp, Jonathan decided to visit a certain old man, the grandfather of the boys who had invited Jonathan to camp. The two families occasionally visited each other. Jonathan had once heard him speak in a church and had felt rather vaguely that here was someone who knew God. He was a gentle old man with kind blue eyes, and Jonathan felt he might be able to talk to him. He phoned him up and was invited over to tea.

Jonathan felt rather nervous as he cycled to the gate, unsure of what he would say, or even if there was anything to say. But the old man was very welcoming and drew up two chairs in front of the blazing old-fashioned coal fire, while his wife brought in tea. Comforted by the warmth and the hot buttered toast, Jonathan found that he could discuss his troubles quite easily, and they talked for a long time.

Then, suddenly, the old man said, "What about your church? Its members should be helping you and praying for you. Have you talked all this over with your vicar or pastor?"

Jonathan looked embarrassed. At last he said, "Well, to be honest, I don't usually go to church. My family only goes at Christmas and Easter, and Sunday is a very busy day for me. I'm studying for O level examinations, and I need the weekends to get on with other things. Besides, I did go once or twice, and I found it rather boring. I try and read my Bible a bit extra on Sundays, and sometimes I go for a walk in the country, but I haven't done anything about church."

The old man seemed to be thinking. Then he took up the tongs, leaned forward, picked one glowing coal out of the fire, and laid it carefully by itself on the grate. "Watch that coal," he said quietly. "Tell me what happens to it."

Jonathan stared at the white-hot, glowing particle and saw the glow fade under his eyes. Red gave way to dull gray, and the light disappeared and the heat grew cold. Then the old man picked the coal up again and put it back into the blaze. "Watch it again," he said. Soon the dull gray lump was kindled, caught alight, and became part of the glowing heart of the fire.

Then the old man explained that Christians were never meant to go it alone, any more than one coal can keep a fire going alone, or a soldier can fight a war alone, or a hand or a foot can function alone. "The soldier is part of an army, and the hand is part of a body. When you became a Christian, you became part of a body—the real church. This body consists of all people in every country who love Jesus, but who, for convenience sake, meet in different buildings and worship in different ways. They are nevertheless all one in the eyes of God. By yourself you are at risk of growing cold, but gathered with other Christians—learning, sharing, giving, and praying together—your faith will be strengthened, your love will grow warm, and your light will shine."

As Jonathan cycled home that night he decided not to let another Sunday pass without finding a church where people loved Jesus and learned together and prayed together, for he had realized his need of getting back into the heart of the fire.

Some people enjoy company more than others. You might be a loner rather than a sociable person and therefore may tend to feel shy and uneasy in a group of people. You will still be greatly helped in your Christian life by becoming a part of some form of Christian group—a youth group, Sunday school, or church fellowship. Perhaps it will not be easy to start with; it might even take several weeks before you begin to relax and enjoy it. But if you stick to it, you will meet and befriend others with whom you have much in common. You will share faith in Jesus as well as many of the same questions, problems, and joys. You will find help and be able to help those around you.

Scripture

Let us not give up the habit of meeting together, as some are doing. Hebrews 10:25

(A prayer of Jesus) "I pray that they may all be one. Father! May they be in us, just as you are in me and I am in you. May they be one, so that the world will believe that you sent me." John 17:21

Prayer

Father, I pray for my church and for all those who teach and preach there. Help me to be faithful and regular in going to the services, and help me to use Sunday rightly, remembering that it is your special day. I pray that week by week I may learn more about you and that I too may be a reliable member of my church. Please show me what I can do to help it.

Reflection

You will personally benefit from joining a Christian group, but remember also that by doing so you can be a help and encouragement to others.

Chapter 43

God protects and shelters us

Psalms 27; 91

THE MATCHBOX AND THE COIN

A girl of twelve lived in a country where Christians were abused and persecuted. She was thinking of becoming a Christian, but she could not stop worrying about the consequences. "If I follow Christ, can I be sure that he will keep me safe and protect me from harm?" she wondered.

Her friend picked up an empty matchbox and slipped a silver coin inside it. "Look," said her friend. "The matchbox is like your body; the silver coin is like your spirit. If I fling this matchbox on the floor, what happens to the silver piece?"

"Nothing. It will not be hurt."

"And if I scrunch up the box in my hand?"

"Well, the matchbox will break, but the silver coin will stay undamaged in your hand."

"If I throw it in the fire?"

"The matchbox will burn . . . but not the coin, I don't think. You could take it out again."

"And which would you say is the more precious and important?"

"The silver coin, of course."

"So in the same way, you can commit your body and spirit into the hands of Jesus, day by day. Your body may sometimes get hurt, and one day it will die. But the real you, the important part of you, will never die. In the hands of the Lord Jesus you will be kept safe from fear and sin."

The Lord is able to protect us and keep us safe. No one can separate us from him, and nothing can hurt our bodies without God—in his love—allowing it.

Scripture

[Jesus said,] "I have told you this so that you will have peace by being united to me. The world will make you suffer. But be brave! I have defeated the world!" John 16:33

Even if I go through the deepest darkness, I will not be afraid, Lord, for you are with me. Psalm 23:4

Prayer

Lord, I know that you want my total commitment to you. I know, too, that you want the very best for all of us. But I am afraid. I am frightened of pain and suffering or of being different. I am frightened of what you might ask of me. Please help me to trust you more and to really believe that anything that happens to me, you have allowed out of love.

Reflection

To what extent does your faith in God and your love for him change with good and bad circumstances?

THE GUARD THEY DARED NOT KILL

Nearly a hundred years ago, as a young man, Upton Westcott went to Zaire to preach the gospel to people who in those days lived as cannibals. His time in Zaire was full of struggle: his wife died of black-water fever, and Upton became blind. But still he stayed on, directing and organizing what by then had become a large and flourishing mission. And eventually, among the people he loved, he died.

On a rare visit to England, the white-haired Westcott told this story. It was hard to tell that the old man was blind—he walked so erect and fearlessly.

His eyes seemed to be looking back to those years long ago when the story took place.

Westcott and his friends had pitched their tent near a cluster of huts not far from a lake. It was a beautiful stretch of water but infested with hippos and crocodiles. Behind the tent was the mysterious green border of the jungle. The people they met brought them bananas and other fruit, and when they had finished their hoeing and fishing of an evening, the villagers would come to squat round the fire and listen to what the young men had to tell them. Gradually a few came to realize that this message of love and eternal life was for them, too. One by one they turned from heathen practices to belief in Jesus and learned to live as Christians should—with honesty and peace, caring for one another.

They were very brave, those African converts, for their lives had been haunted by evil spirits, and it was hard to believe that this new, loving Father could really keep them safe. There was one witch doctor whom they had always especially feared. His charms and magic were supposed to take effect over a great area. He was reported to be very angry when he heard that his people were turning to the true and living God, and all waited anxiously to see what his revenge would be.

One day at suppertime the kraal was busy with its fires and bubbling clay pots, and Upton and his two friends were also cooking, when they saw a frightened boy beckoning to them from the margin of the jungle. The men went to speak to him and found that he was trembling and his eyes were full of fear. "I have come to warn you," he whispered. "You must escape tonight. My father will help you. He has a canoe ready, and you must be down by the creek before the moon rises tonight. He says it is your only chance."

"But why should we flee? Who is going to harm us?"

"Why, the Great Witch Doctor. Tonight he sends his killers. At the darkest hour they will attack with spears. You cannot escape them."

The three men held a quick consultation. They had a gun for shooting wild beasts, but they did not intend to use it for killing people. Besides, what use would it be if the tent was surrounded by spear throwers? Westcott and his friends had taught these young men and women to rely on God's protection, so they, the Christian missionaries, could not run away even if they had a place to run to. Westcott turned back to the frightened, waiting boy.

"Thank your father," he said. "But tell him that our God has not told us to flee. We will trust his protection and wait for what comes."

The boy sped off, and the three made ready for bed. They ate their supper as usual, and the tropical night came swiftly. Never had they been so conscious of the rustle of leaves, snakes, and birds or the soft distant chatter of monkeys. They sat for a time in the door of their tent, praying and waiting.

The moon rose, and the world was flooded with silver light, but the three had no desire to go and lie down in the tent. Better, they thought, to meet death in the open, seeing their enemies, than to be cornered like rats in a trap. All night they waited under the fierce tropical stars. Then the moon set. It was the cold, eerie hour when mists rise from the lake and the world is shrouded. Perhaps now?

But no one came. When at last the sun rose, the tired young men, who had never expected to see another dawn on earth, watched the mists scatter with new eyes. Then came the sound of voices at the well, the crackling of fuel, the thud of hoes, and the wreaths of smoke rising from the kraal. Never had life seemed so beautiful! They crawled into their tents and slept soundly.

The little group of Christians, creeping up and peering fearfully through the tent flaps, praised God and wondered, for had they not heard the news of the planned attack and mourned as those who had lost a father? Surely, the hand of the Lord sheltered these teachers.

Months passed, and because no harm came to those who no longer worshiped the spirits, others took heart. Love and freedom were far better than the old bondage of fear. Besides, the old witch doctor seemed to have lost his power. Some said that he was too old, and others said that the spirits had forsaken him. Whatever the reason, men feared him no more.

But all the same, Westcott was very surprised one day to find the old witch doctor kneeling in the doorway of his tent, his finery drooping, his monkey tails flapping. When at last he bowed himself in, Westcott saw that he looked weak and hollow-eyed. "I want to learn about the living God," he said simply.

The two talked for a long time. Westcott spoke to him of sin and repentance, and he seemed uneasy. There was so much sin . . . and there was one sin that weighed heavier on his conscience than any other.

"Then confess it, that it may be forgiven," said Westcott.

So he told all. It was the night of the new moon, he explained, and he had sent his men through the jungle with spears and orders to kill the three foreigners. But they came back with their spears clean. They had shed no blood.

"But why?" asked Westcott. "We were unarmed. No one could have prevented them."

"It was because there were four of you," said the witch doctor. "My men had no order to kill four, and they could not see who was who. They waited till the mists rose, but the fourth man did not go away. My friend, who was that man who sat with you all the night in the moonlight?"

Westcott could not answer that question. Had the Lord himself sat with them, or had he sent his angel? He did not know. It was enough for him that they had seen the morning and that the old witch doctor himself was turning to the light of the Lord Jesus.

Scripture

His angel guards those who honor the Lord and rescues them from danger. Psalm 34:7

Even if I go through the deepest darkness, I will not be afraid, Lord, for you are with me. Your shepherd's rod and staff protect me. Psalm 23:4

Prayer

Thank you, Lord, for your continual care over me, all day and all night. Thank you for any time in my life when I have been ill or in danger and you have saved and protected me.

Keep by your love and power any who are in danger tonight, any I know in countries at war, and any who are unjustly imprisoned because they are Christians. Help them to know that whatever happens, nothing can separate them from the love of Christ. May your love take away their fear, and may they be comforted and strengthened. Give them peace and courage today.

Reflection

It is sometimes difficult to trust and praise God in spite of dangerous or painful circumstances. Make a collection of the many stories like Westcott's, including ones from the Bible and ones from your own life, as constant reminders that God is our rescuer.

Chapter 45

In a crisis God gives us the supernatural wisdom we need

Matthew 10:16-42

THE HILL THEY COULD NOT CLIMB

During the civil war in Rwanda in the 1960s, members of one tribe rose up against another tribe and marched through the countryside armed with axes, hoes, and knives, killing and burning the thatched kraals. Inside the hospital precincts on one hilltop an African pastor and his wife and two English nurses, Doreen and Jo, were faced with a dilemma during that time. One day they had looked over the plain and seen little columns of smoke rising in the distance. They slept uneasily and woke early the next morning to see the glow of the flames in a ring round the bottom of the hill. They knew that the murderers were very close.

Should they shelter the refugees from the burning kraals or not? To do so would be to take sides against the armed rebels, and almost certainly to bring the whole band up the hill to plunder and murder not only the refugees but probably the hospital patients and staff as well. To refuse the refugees, however, could also mean death to the crowd of nearly three hundred terrified people already swarming up the hill carrying little children and anything else they had managed to snatch from the flames. Could this Christian hospital shut its doors and send them all back to the murderous valley and the fires? They decided that they could not, and the weeping, exhausted mob surged in to lodge in every corner of the house, the hospital, and the church.

Now, however, all in the hospital area were in real danger, and a meeting of the staff was called. They decided that the African pastor and nurse Jo should leave in the car, under cover of darkness, and try to get through to find help. The pastor's wife, Edreda, and nurse Doreen should stay and face what came. Together they four prayed for God's protection over the two in the car, for wisdom for the two left behind, and for safety for the terrified crowds in the hospital. Then Doreen remembered a small picture that had recently been given her. It was a painting of a flock of sheep, some white and some black, with an angry, snarling wolf trying to attack them. But between the sheep and the wolf was a pierced hand stretched out, and nothing could get past that pierced hand.

As darkness fell, the car set out to pick its way through the burning home-

144

steads and rebel bands. Doreen was busy trying to calm the fears of her hundreds of guests and to make them as comfortable and welcome as possible. At last, worn out, she went to bed. On waking next morning, she ran to the window, and there, sure enough, was the rabble army about to climb the hill—a terrifying mob of wild, armed men out for blood.

She had no idea what to do. The only possible course seemed persuasion. She called Edreda, and together they walked down the hill to meet the rebels. The men, amazed at such a show of fearlessness, halted.

Doreen spoke to them, explaining that they had no enemies, that their only function was to heal and to tell out the love of God. Politely and firmly the leader replied that that was all very well, but they were harboring enemies, and unless certain men were handed over by nightfall, they would attack the mission, capture the refugees, and burn the buildings.

The voice that answered him seemed to Doreen to belong to someone else. Astonished and unafraid, she heard herself saying, "You cannot come up this hill. It is God's hill."

A moment of stunned silence followed, and then a boy, his eyes blazing with hate, thrust his face close to hers and shouted, "There is no God, Mademoiselle."

"Oh, yes, there is," she heard herself saying. "And you will see that he will not allow you to climb this hill. He is going to protect us."

There was an angry muttering and a forward surge as some tried to push past her, but the Hand was stretched out. The bandits faltered and fell back, and Doreen and Edreda turned and climbed the hill alone.

The danger, however, was not yet over. They gathered the refugees and told them of the threats, advising as many as possible to try and slip away when dusk fell and make for the Ugandan border. Then they prayed, and a great silence fell over the restless, frightened crowd as once again they claimed God's protection. Suddenly the silence was broken by the tap of raindrops on galvanized iron roofs. Soon the rain was coming down in torrents. Mass attack through the liquid mud of the hillside would be impossible, and some on the hilltop began to sing for joy.

Later in the evening, a bedraggled car chugged up the road through the floods and darkness. The pastor and Jo had got through and returned with authority to call on the militia to protect them. For the moment they were safe, and a few days later the refugees would be slipped into government lorries and escorted over the Ugandan border to safety.

Scripture

A promise for those who are not sure how to act:

If any of you is lacking in wisdom, ask God, who gives to all generously and ungrudgingly, and it will be given you. James 1:5, NRSV

A promise for those who suddenly find themselves questioned about their beliefs:

When they bring you to trial, do not worry about what you are going to say or how you will say it; when the time comes, you will be given what you will say. For the words you will speak will not be yours; they will come from the Spirit of your Father speaking through you. Matthew 10:19-20

Prayer

Lord, when I am in difficult situations and do not know how to act, give me your wisdom. When I have an opportunity to speak for you and do not know what to say, give me your words. Thank you that you are always there. Please keep me in close contact with you so that I can ask for your help at any moment I need you.

Reflection

Even human beings' greatest strength is only weakness compared to the hand of God. Watch for ways you see God's hand protecting you and his wisdom guiding you.

Chapter 46

THE BRIGHTER LIGHT

God brings good out of all circumstances

Romans 8:28

Like many shepherd boys, Mikhail may have longed for more schooling and adventure, for a shepherd's life in the hills of Lebanon was not a very interesting one. But Mikhail was needed to lead the flock to pasture every morning, guard it through the long hours of the day, and lead it home at night. This was how the boy spent much of his childhood and would, no doubt, have spent much of the rest of his life had tragedy not struck him.

It seemed a perfectly ordinary day. Mikhail was wandering idly about while the flock grazed when he noticed a smooth shiny object half hidden by foliage and stooped down to examine it. Was it a smooth stone? He picked it up, and what happened next he probably does not remember, for he had picked up an unexploded bomb. The next thing he knew was pain and darkness—many people hurrying round him, but always darkness, so that he could not tell if it was night or day.

At last, when he came round and was able to think properly, he realized that he was in a hospital. Gradually it dawned on him that it was going to be pitch-dark for the rest of his life, for the bomb had destroyed both his eyes. He also realized that he had lost his right hand, but this loss probably seemed small compared with the loss of his sight. Mikhail felt he would never, never get over it and longed to die. When they took him home, he lay down with his face to the wall and took no notice of anyone.

Visitors came in plenty to sympathize over the accident, and, although he would barely speak to them, he could hardly help hearing what they said. But nothing really interested Mikhail until one day two ladies arrived who were strangers. They said, "We have come to offer Mikhail a place at the Blind School in Beirut," and went on to talk about this extraordinary school. Boys there apparently learned to read and work with their hands. It almost sounded as though they were happy.

Mikhail lay slumped in his corner, appearing to take no notice but actually listening to every word. It all sounded nonsense to him. How could a blind boy read and work and be happy? Blind boys lay with their faces to the wall and waited for life to end. There was nothing they could do. So the visitors left, but as they said good-bye they added quietly, "If he will come, we promise him a place."

Some time passed, and the subject of school was not mentioned again. Mikhail thought of it nearly all the time, though; in his long night there was nothing much else to think about. Gradually he came to realize that by giving it a try he had nothing to lose. So one day he astonished his parents by turning round and saying, "That Blind School in Beirut! You'd better take me there. That's where I want to go."

They made ready, and he and his parents traveled down from the hills to the great city by the sea. Walking through the crowded streets, they found the address and knocked on the door. All three must have felt terribly nervous, but they were very courteously received and taken to a waiting room. As they passed through, the parents caught glimpses of boys making baskets and caning chairs, and boys studying, their fingers moving over the pages of great books. And, yes, they even looked happy! It was all most strange.

The master of the school came to see them and listened to their story, but he looked very sadly at the silent boy who sat so still. When he had heard all they had to say, he shook his head sorrowfully. "It is impossible," he said. "You have come too late. All the places are full."

But he had not judged the quiet boy accurately. Mikhail suddenly looked up. "You promised!" he cried bitterly. "You *promised!*" And he pleaded, weeping, for a chance. Finally, seeing that the boy was desperate, the master promised to fit him in somehow.

That was how Mikhail started off on what was to become his lifework, for he himself is now the headmaster of the Blind School. From the beginning he refused to let his handicap hinder him. He learned Braille reading almost as soon as the others, using only his left hand. Basket making was a problem at first, but he overcame it by tucking the cane under his right arm. Watching Mikhail's expression gradually change from dull despair to bright intelligence over time, the master often thanked God that he had accepted this eager, hardworking boy.

One evening, years later, the boys were gathered in the hall listening to a Bible talk. When it was over, the speaker asked if any of the boys would like to share something that he had learned. Mikhail rose to his feet. "I want to thank God for my blindness," he said simply. "Without it, I should never have known the Light of the World."

———— ❖◦❉◦❖ ————

All of us wonder at times why God allows trouble and disappointments to come into our lives, and why innocent people have to suffer. I once stood in a carpet factory and watched the children, sitting cross-legged in front of the looms, weave carpets that are famous all over the world. By each child's side lay a pile of bright-colored threads and, surprisingly, a pile of dull, dark threads—and their swift little fingers used both. When I went round to the other side of the loom and saw the beautiful pattern unfolding, I understood why they needed both threads. The design would have been ruined without the dark background.

Someone once wrote this verse, which helps give an answer to our questions about the pain God allows:

> Not till the loom is silent, and the shuttles cease to fly,
> Will God unroll the canvas and explain the reason why.
> The dark threads are as needful in the weaver's skillful hand
> As the threads of gold and silver in the pattern he has planned.

Scripture

We know that in all things God works for good with those who love him. Romans 8:28

Prayer

Lord, thank you for the things you send into my life that seem hard and disappointing. Help me to believe that they, too, are part of the pattern. Keep me from grumbling and doubting. Keep me joyful and praising because I trust you.

Reflection

Can you look back to an unpleasant or painful event in your life and see now that a great good has come out of it?

Chapter 47 — BORN TO FLY

*We will be raised
to life again*

1 Corinthians 15

"Come on," said the robin kindly. "Can't you move a little quicker? The sun is shining on those leaves. I suppose you can't climb any higher, but at least you could feel its warmth on your back."

"Yes," agreed the caterpillar, eating its way slowly through a nettle leaf, "I do enjoy the warmth. But as the sun occasionally shines in the ditch, I see no reason to go higher. I'm perfectly content with my quarters, and there are some very good leaves down here."

"Ditches! Leaves!" trilled the robin. "If only you knew! Don't you ever long for sunlight and waving treetops and blue skies and birdsong and white clouds and wind?"

"Not really, dear," said the caterpillar. "I'm sure it's all very nice. But I've always preferred green to blue, and I never did like the wind. As for swaying trees, I'd much rather keep still. It's far safer."

The robin laughed. "Well, I suppose you can't help it," he said gaily. "But, oh, I'm so glad, so very glad that I was born with wings." He soared to the top of a swaying ash tree and perched there, singing and singing and singing.

The caterpillar reared herself up on her hind segments and listened for a long time. The happy song drifted down to her through the leaves. *Wings!* she thought to herself. *I wonder . . .* Her body suddenly felt tired and heavy and the boundaries of her sight very near. *But I wasn't born for treetops and wide skies and the open spaces they talk about. . . . I don't even know what they look like. I was born for ditches and nettles and low plants. It's not a bad life either, while it lasts.*

She continued to munch at her leaf and tried to feel content, but she was in a strange, restless mood. *I must be getting old*, she mused, *or I wouldn't be feeling like this. Wings . . . wings!*

There was a tiny movement just above her, and she looked up to see a butterfly perched on a Michaelmas daisy for an airy moment, the sunshine filtering through her wings. Thinking she had never seen anything so light and beautiful, the caterpillar suddenly became painfully conscious of her own heavy body. The butterfly alighted right on her half-munched nettle, and she forgot herself completely in the love and beauty of her visitor. "Where have you come from?" she whispered. "You don't belong to the ditch."

"Neither do you," laughed the butterfly. "You're only a visitor here. You were born for the light, for wings and air and blue skies. I came to tell you."

"I don't know what you're talking about," gasped the caterpillar. "And yet . . . sometimes I do have a strange feeling that I'm a stranger in this ditch. There's something else . . . but surely I, with my slow, heavy body, could never be like you. How could this ever be?"

"It doesn't appear yet what you will be," breathed the butterfly. "But I know that you are going to be like me. Don't forget. You weren't born for the ditch. It's only part of the journey. You were born to fly. . . ."

Her voice could be heard no longer for her wings had lifted her out of sight, and the caterpillar was left desolate, longing for wings. She tried to munch several leaves, but they were dull and tasteless. Nothing seemed to comfort her. By evening she was worn out and curled up in the ditch that had been her home all her life. *I have a strange feeling that I shan't be here much longer,* she thought just before she fell asleep. *There's somewhere else!*

The caterpillar slept and slept and slept. She wove a soft cocoon round herself that hardened into a chrysalis, and the rain and the falling autumn leaves covered her. Her neighbors in the ditch, the field mouse and the hedgehog and a whole commune of small earwigs, thought that she had died, and they were sorry, for she had been a pleasant, well-behaved little caterpillar. They missed her.

But she was not dead, not in the least! In her sleep one day she had a most extraordinary dream. Something was calling her far, far away, but very urgently, like the chime of happy distant bells. She was imprisoned, though, and could not respond. *I could never struggle out of this prison with my poor, soft, strengthless body,* she thought. *And yet, if I don't answer this call, I know that I shall die.*

And then she discovered she was not dreaming at all. She was struggling with a strength she had never possessed before, and her shackles were breaking. She was pushing out into light and warmth and birdsong. She could not understand her own strength. It was like being born again. "I'm different," she whispered. "My body is no longer heavy and slow. That call is somewhere far above me, but I am rising. I used to think that I should feel strange if I rose too far above the ditch, but I am no stranger to this sweet air. I feel completely fulfilled. . . . This is what I was born for."

She paused to rest on a bluebell, and a charming blue butterfly joined her. "Welcome to our company," he remarked. "I see your wings are scarcely unfolded. Allow me to show you the way to the buddleia tree. We are all over there."

"Wings!" The little caterpillar nearly swooned. Who and what had she become? She felt shy in the presence of this beautiful stranger and fluttered awkwardly to the edge of a birdbath. Without knowing what she was doing, she glanced down into the water and caught sight of her own reflection. She saw a magnificent red admiral with dark wings and red spots.

"Born to fly," she whispered. "Born for the light!" And, stretching her wings to full capacity, she followed her bright guide to join the company of other creatures like her.

Scripture

This is how it will be when the dead are raised to life. When the body is buried, it is mortal; when raised, it will be immortal. When buried, it is ugly and weak; when raised, it will be beautiful and strong. When buried, it is a physical body; when raised, it will be a spiritual body. . . . We shall all be changed. 1 Corinthians 15:42-44,51

Just as we are like the one who was made out of earth, we will be like the one who came from heaven. 1 Corinthians 15:49, CEV

Prayer

Thank you, Lord, for the joy and strength and beauty of those who have died trusting in Jesus, and thank you for the day when we shall all meet again.

Reflection

Jesus Christ is the turning point of history, for he died, rose from the dead, and showed himself alive again to men and women. . . . So death is not really the end. It is a new beginning.

Chapter 48

FOOTSTEPS IN THE NIGHT

*Jesus will return
someday and take us
to be with him*

Matthew 24:32-51

The master was going away, and nobody quite knew why. The servants had plenty to talk about. The master was young and unmarried, and some whispered that he intended to return with a bride. Others thought that he was off on some business deal that might take him overseas, for his wool, his wine, and his wheat were well known all over. One thing only was sure, and that was that it would be a fairly long absence. He had given the bailiff exact instructions about the shearing and the harvesting, so he apparently intended to be away all summer. He had also talked to the head of the vinedressers about repairing the winepress and storing the vats, so he would probably not return till the early autumn. He had of course given clear directions about running the house as well. Everyone knew his job and would carry on as usual.

The master left on a bright spring morning, promising to come back soon, and the servants watched him ride down the valley with mixed feelings. He was a kind, just master, and they all respected him. At the same time, he was a stickler for work, and some of them rather liked the prospect of slacking off for a time. The bailiff was inclined to be lazy himself when the master was away, never bothering too much about how things were done. The workers wandered back to their jobs rather more slowly than usual.

Only one among them fought back his tears as he watched the tall, strong figure disappear from view among the cypress trees. Fidelis had been born a slave and had grown up in the power of a very evil master where he was overworked, half-starved, and often savagely flogged. His present master had once come to the evil master's house to trade and had caught sight of the child. Fidelis had never forgotten the look of mingled compassion and fury that had burned in the visitor's eyes as he gazed at his scarred body and terrified expression. The master had immediately asked to buy the boy and paid a fantastic price for his freedom, since Fidelis, young and good-looking, was reckoned a valuable slave. Then he had lifted the trembling child up onto the horse in front of him with very gentle hands and comforted him with such reassuring words that by the time they arrived home, Fidelis already loved his rescuer.

A deep, steady love had then grown with the years. Fidelis swept the yards, looked after the watchdogs, and slept near the great front door in case travelers arrived by night—quite a humble job. But he worked for love of his master, and the joy of his life was to serve him and be near him, so Fidelis was usually happy.

Well, he could still serve him while he was gone. The weeks would pass quickly if he worked hard, and when the master returned he would find the yards spotless and the dogs in fighting-fit, bouncing condition. Fidelis rolled up his sleeves and set to with such energy that the cook burst out laughing. "Bless the boy!" she shouted. "Anyone would think the master was coming back tonight!"

The time really did pass quickly. The sheep were sheared somehow, the harvest gathered, and the wine pressed. When summer was nearly over, Fidelis often walked far down the valley in the cool of the evening, just in case . . . Surely the master would come soon! He did not much care for the servants' quarters these days. Everyone was quarreling and grumbling and gossiping about the master's long absence. The bailiff himself was seldom seen outside during working hours, and it was whispered that he had moved into his master's private apartment and was entertaining his friends with his master's old wine.

The poplars turned gold and the first rains fell on the parched land, and still the master did not come. It was then that the rumors started. With travelers on the roads so few, it was generally accepted that he would not come till spring, if at all. Some said that he had gone overseas, and certainly no fool would cross the ocean now that the storms had set in. Others thought he had been attacked by brigands. All were gloomy and depressed, and, now that the grape harvest was over and the wine vatted, those in charge became lazy and drunken. Everyone did as he pleased and worked for his own ends. Only Fidelis remembered and worked for love.

Then one day there was an interesting announcement. The bailiff was inviting everyone to a banquet in the main hall. It was some kind of a celebration. No one knew what there was to celebrate, but they supposed they would be told. *Perhaps*, thought Fidelis, *he will announce the return of the master*. He arrived at the banquet bright-eyed with hope and excitement.

He looked round in amazement at the loaded trestles. Two of his master's sheep had been killed and stewed in honey, and the piles of sweetmeats and confectioneries were surely made from his master's supplies. Then the bailiff rose and hammered on the table. Amidst a deathly silence he announced that news had reached him of the master's death and that this banquet was a take-over. He was inviting them all to celebrate their new allegiance to himself.

Fortunately, Fidelis was sitting at the bottom of the table with the lowest of the menials, so no one saw him hurry from the room. He ran to his little straw pallet near the front door and wept and wept till he could weep no longer. Sensing his misery, the great fierce watchdogs came and lay down beside him, nuzzling him, and this was a comfort, for they, at least, had loved the master. The noise from the hall grew louder as the night wore on and the servants emptied flagon after flagon, but Fidelis lay facedown and desolate, trying to decide what to do next. Never, never would he transfer his allegiance.

Then, suddenly, the great hound at his side tensed, and the one at his feet growled and lifted his head. Fidelis sat up and listened. He could hear nothing but the shouts of drunken laughter from the hall. Then, the dogs started barking madly and made for the door. Fidelis seized their collars and tried to restrain them, but his hands were not strong enough. The dogs had heard that familiar, light, firm step, and they knew who was coming. Out they streaked into the full moonlight and leaped upon the tall figure standing by his horse in the courtyard, and then Fidelis knew, too. He ran forward and stood looking up at his master, his heart too full for speech.

"Down, boys!" cried the master. "Quiet now!" And the dogs crouched and wagged their tails furiously.

Then he looked down into the white, tear-stained face lifted to his and knew immediately that something was very wrong. "Why, Fidelis," he began kindly, "is there only you to welcome me home? What is all this noise that I hear, and why are the lights lit in the hall? And where are the other servants?"

"They are having a banquet, master," whispered Fidelis. "They thought that you were dead." And he sank down on the mounting block and buried his face in his hands.

When the master spoke, his voice was sad and grave. "How comes it, boy, that you alone are not at the banquet?"

And then Fidelis found his tongue. There in the quiet moonlight he poured out his heart. "Didn't you pay that great price for me, master, and make me your servant? And didn't you promise to come back? How could I swear allegiance to another? Don't I belong to you, master? Am I not your servant forever?"

Fidelis thought that one of the dogs had laid its nose on his head, but then he realized that it was the master's hand resting on his hair.

"You are not a servant, Fidelis, but a son forever," said the master. "Come, let us go in."

It often seems as though evil reigns in the world; people have forgotten that Jesus promised to come back. Yet he gave many signs regarding his return, which have been recorded in the New Testament. Enough of these have been fulfilled for many Christians to think that the coming of Jesus is very near.

Scripture

[Jesus said,] "After I go and prepare a place for you, I will come back and take you to myself, so that you will be where I am." John 14:3

So then, you also must always be ready, because the Son of Man will come at an hour when you are not expecting him. Matthew 24:44

He who gives his testimony to all this says, "Yes indeed! I am coming soon!" So be it. Come, Lord Jesus! Revelation 22:20

Prayer

Thank you, Lord Jesus, for the promise you gave us that you would come back and take your children home. Even though I do not know when this will be, teach me to live as one who is ready and waiting for your coming. Thank you for the wonderful happiness we shall know when we see you.

Reflection

As a Christian, ask God to help you be as diligent as if Christ were to return today, and as persevering as if he were to return in a thousand years.

A+ books ™

Counting Books

Flowers
and
Showers

A Spring Counting Book

by Rebecca Fjelland Davis

Reading Consultant: Jennifer Norford
Senior Consultant: Mid-Continent for Research and Education

Capstone
press

Mankato, MN

A+ Books are published by Capstone Press,
151 Good Counsel Drive, P.O. Box 669, Mankato, Minnesota 56002.
www.capstonepress.com

1 2 3 4 5 6 11 10 09 08 07 06

Library of Congress Cataloging-in-Publication Data
Davis, Rebecca Fjelland.
   Flowers and showers: a spring counting book / by Rebecca Fjelland Davis.
   p. cm.—(A+ books. Counting books)
   Includes bibliographical references and index.
   ISBN-13: 978-0-7368-5377-4 (hardcover)
   ISBN-10: 0-7368-5377-4 (hardcover)
   1. Counting—Juvenile literature. 2. Spring—Juvenile literature. I. Title. II. Series.
QA113.D384 2006
513.2'11—dc22   2005019118

Credits

Jenny Marks, editor; Ted Williams, designer; Karon Dubke, photographer; Kelly Garvin,
   photo researcher

Photo Credits

Capstone Press/Karon Dubke, cover (all), 2–3 (all), 4–5, 10–11 (all), 12-13 (all), 16–17 (all),
   18–19 (all), 20–21 (all), 22–23 (all), 26–27 (bunnies, eggs, kites), 28, 29
Corbis/Ralph A. Clevenger, 14–15
Getty Images, Inc./Taxi/Jim Cummins, 24–25
Peter Arnold, Inc./Tim Wright, 6–7 (all), 26 (robin)
Photodisc, 8–9

Note to Parents, Teachers, and Librarians

Flowers and Showers uses color photographs and a rhyming nonfiction format to introduce children
to various signs of the spring season while building mastery of basic counting skills. It is designed
to be read aloud to a pre-reader or to be read independently by an early reader. The images help
early readers and listeners understand the text and concepts discussed. The book encourages further
learning by the following sections: Facts about Spring, Words to Know, Read More, Internet Sites,
and Index. Early readers may need assistance using these features.

Sunshine above, then clouds fill the sky.

Weather goes from warm, to wet, to dry.

So many changes in the season called spring.

Let's count together each and every thing.

3

One colorful kite dances in the sky. Hold the string tight and watch it fly.

4

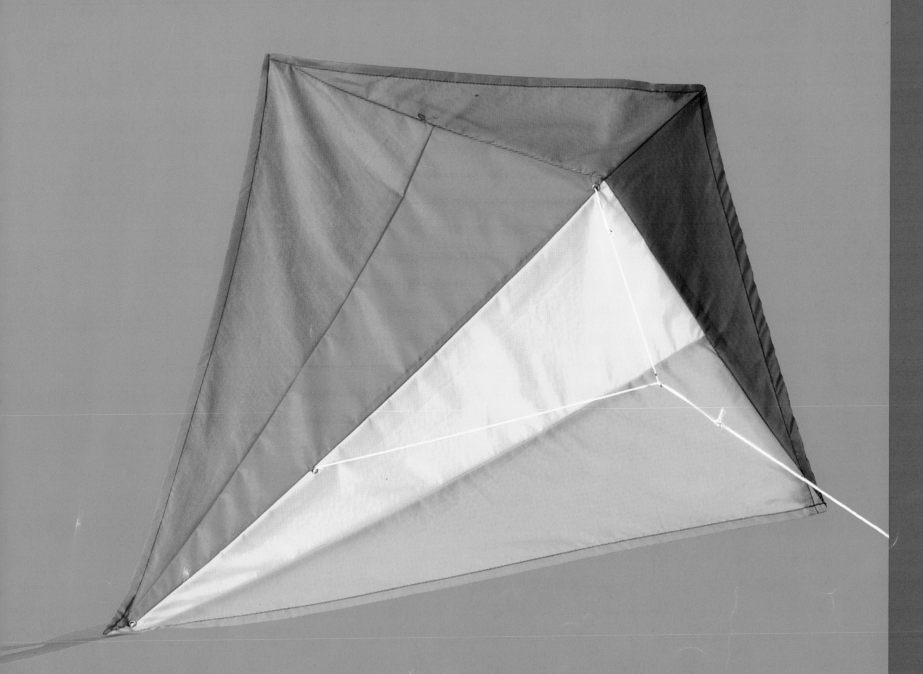

2

Two fat robins, red feathers
on their chests. They come back
in spring to build their nests.

3

Three blue eggs in a robin's batch. Hear the CHIRP! CHIRP! when the babies hatch.

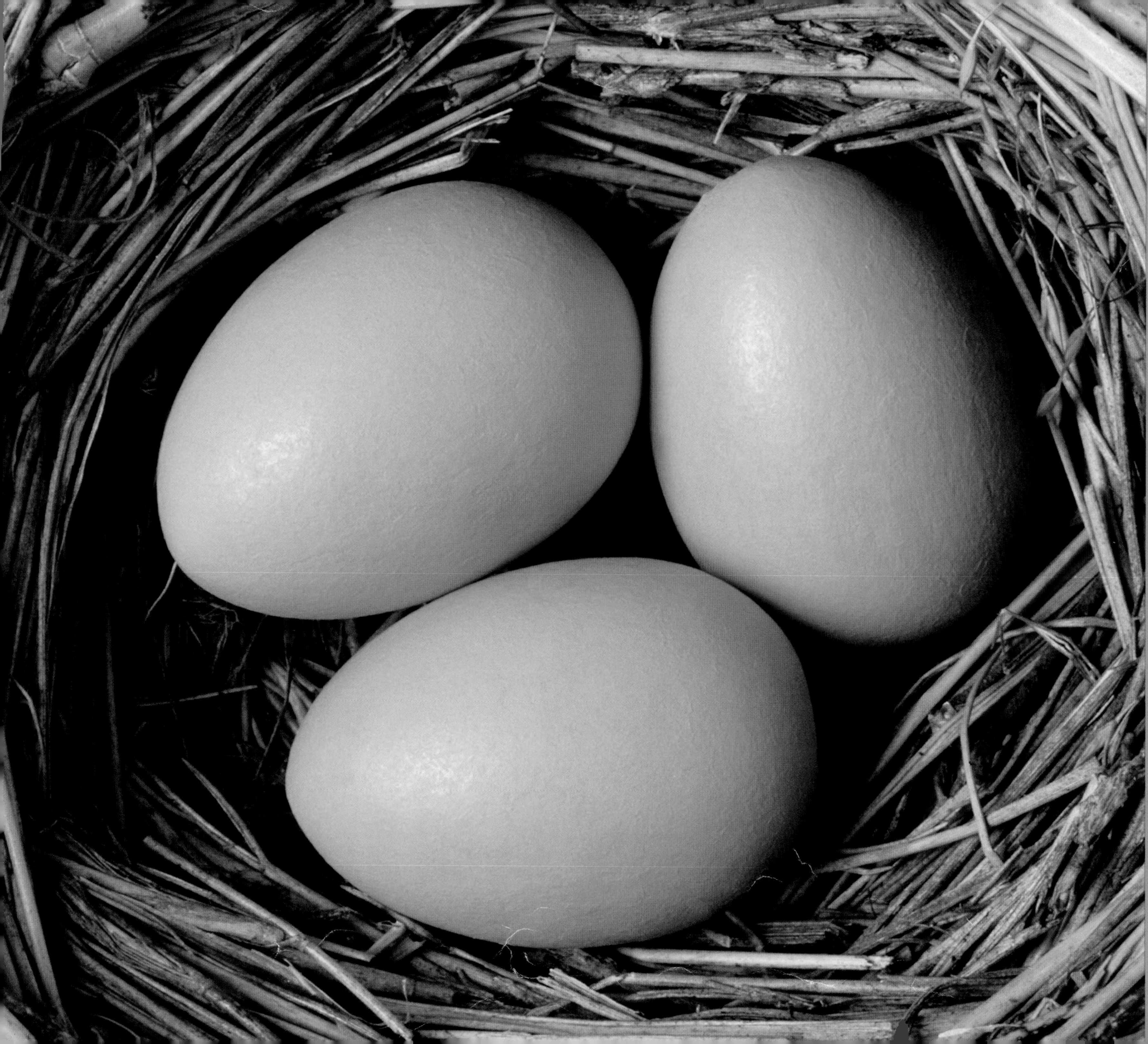

Four striped caterpillars, watch them wiggle by. In spring each becomes a Monarch butterfly.

5

Five little bunnies HOP! HOP! HOP! Munching green grass, they never seem to stop.

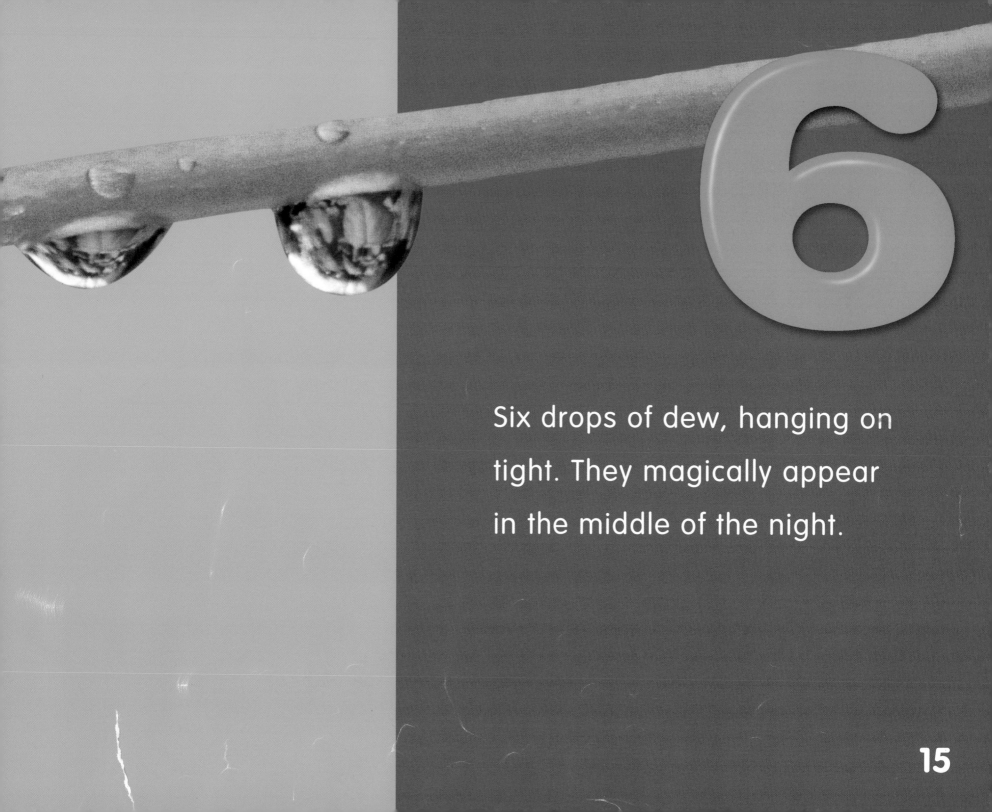

Six drops of dew, hanging on tight. They magically appear in the middle of the night.

Seven bright umbrellas under skies so gray. They'll keep you dry as you walk along your way.

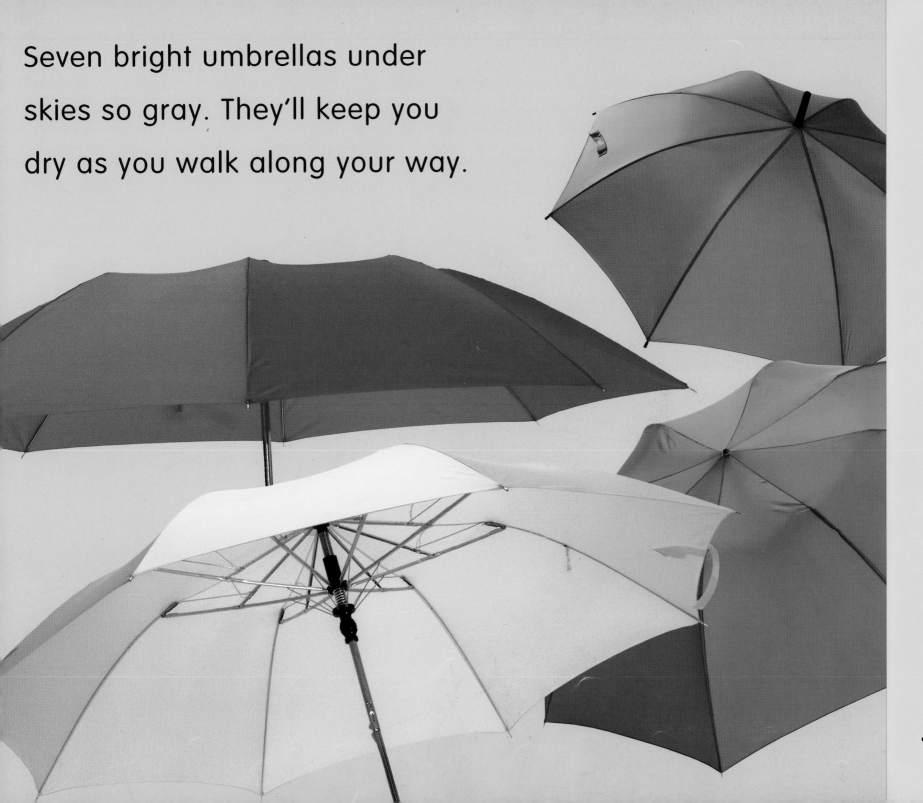

1
2
3
4
5
6
7
8
9
10

Eight bean seeds, so eager to sprout. Count them fast before the roots poke out.

8

19

9

Nine hatched chicks have no time to sleep. Listen to their calls of CHEEP! CHEEP! CHEEP!

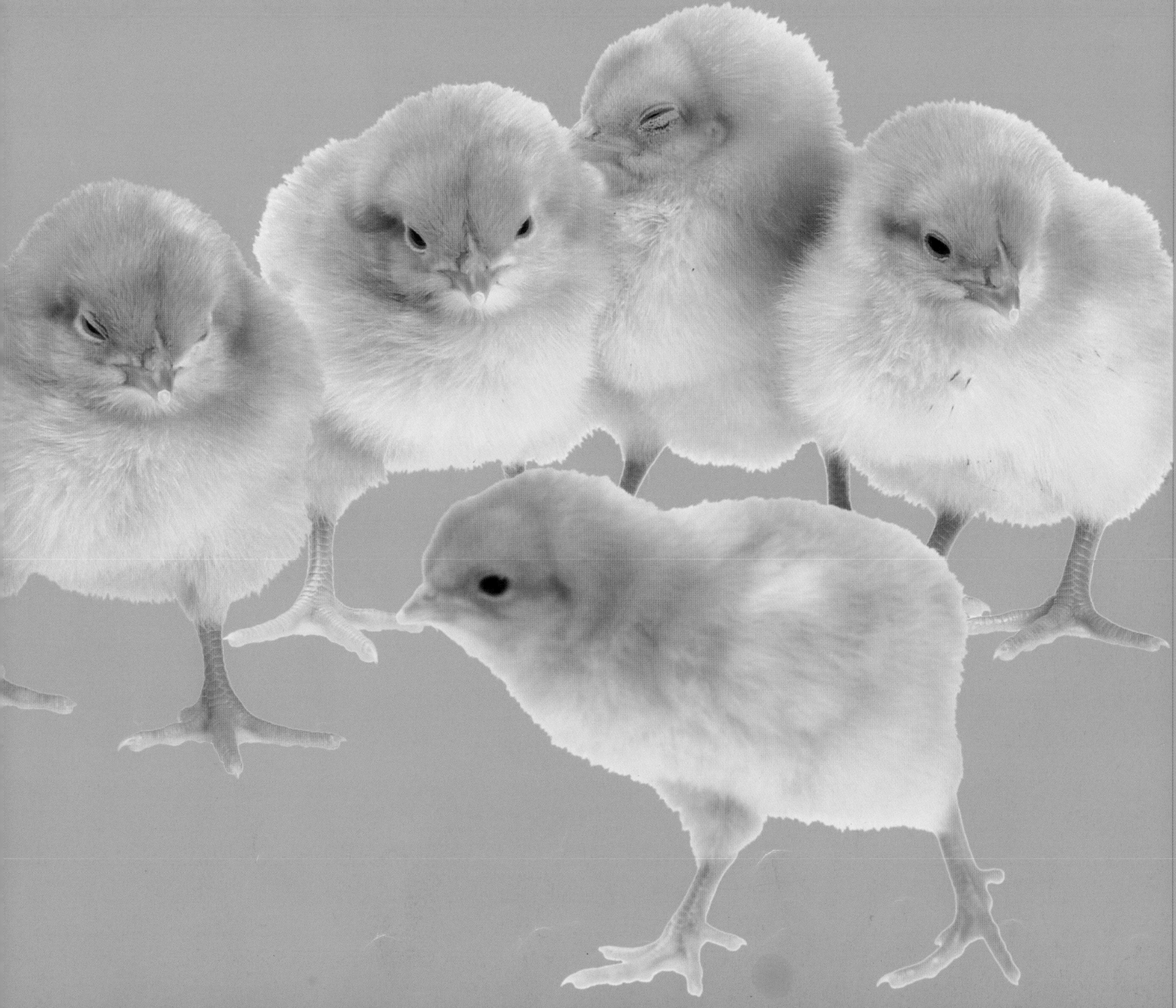

1
2
3
4
5
6
7
8
9
10

10

Ten yellow tulips burst into bloom. Bring them inside to brighten up a room.

Spring is the season of drips, drops, and sun. Don't wait for clear skies—rain can be fun!

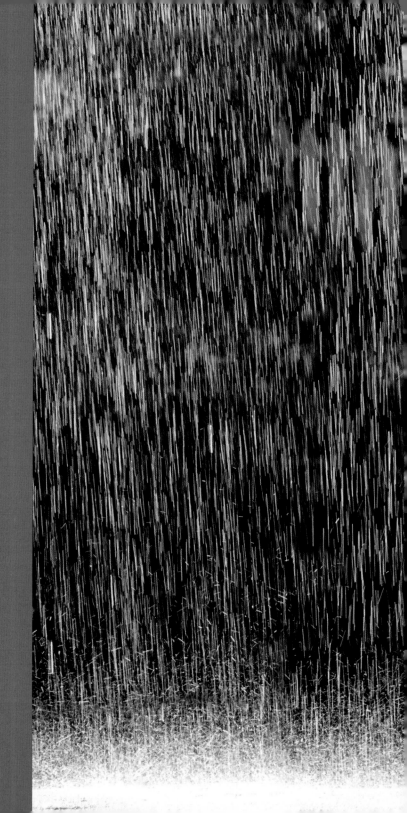

25

How Many?

Robins

Bunnies

Kites

Eggs

27

Facts about Spring

In spring, water from melted snow and rain rushes into rivers. Sometimes this rush of water causes rivers to overflow and flood.

Mother rabbits have an average of ten baby bunnies at a time.

Spring rains bring worms to the surface of the ground. When robins migrate north in spring, they can easily find food to eat.

Most tree buds are waxy. Their waxy surface protects the new leaves growing underneath.

A bean seed has two halves. When it sprouts, each half grows into a leaf.

Kites work much like sails on sailboats. Moving air pushes kites high into the sky.

Caterpillars make cocoons to rest in. While in their cocoons, the caterpillars change into moths or butterflies through a process called metamorphosis.

Fuzzy caterpillars usually turn into moths. Caterpillars that aren't fuzzy usually turn into butterflies.

Words to Know

bud (BUHD)—a small part of a plant that grows into a leaf

bloom (BLOOM)—to have flowers appear on a plant

cocoon (kuh-KOON)—a covering made of silky thread; caterpillars rest in their cocoons while they change into butterflies and moths.

dew (DOO)—small water drops that collect overnight on outside surfaces, such as plants and leaves

flood (FLUHD)—to overflow with water

metamorphosis (met-uh-MOR-fuh-sis)—a series of changes; caterpillars change through metamorphosis to become moths and butterflies.

migrate (MYE-grate)—to move from one place to another when seasons change

season (SEE-zuhn)—one of the four parts of the year; winter, autumn, spring, and summer are seasons.

weather (WETH-ur)—the conditions outside

Read More

Chapman, Cindy. *Baby Animals.* Compass Point Phonics Readers. Minneapolis: Compass Point Books, 2004.

Eckart, Edana. *Watching the Seasons.* Watching Nature. New York: Children's Press, 2004.

Glaser, Linda. *It's Spring.* Celebrate the Seasons! Brookfield, Conn.: Millbrook Press, 2002.

Maurer, Tracy Nelson. *A to Z of Spring.* A to Z. Vero Beach, Fla.: Rourke, 2003.

Internet Sites

FactHound offers a safe, fun way to find Internet sites related to this book. All of the sites on FactHound have been researched by our staff.

Here's how:

1) Visit *www.facthound.com*
2) Type in this special code **0736853774** for age-appropriate sites. Or enter a search word related to this book for a more general search.
3) Click on the **"FETCH IT"** button.

FactHound will fetch the best sites for you!

Index